Did That Just Happen?

Order this book online at www.trafford.com
or email orders@trafford.com

Most Trafford titles are also available at major online book retailers.

Edited by Pam Guerrieri,
Cover Design and Photography by L. M. Yust,
Layout by Daniel Smith.

Print information available on the last page.

ISBN: 978-1-4251-6272-6 (sc)
ISBN: 978-1-4251-8740-8 (hc)

Trafford rev. 06/26/2024

www.trafford.com

North America & international
toll-free: 844-688-6899 (USA & Canada)
fax: 812 355 4082

Did That Just Happen?

(My Personal Collection of)
Supernatural Events

By
L. M. Yust

 # Dedication

In memory of my mother-in-law, Joyce, who opened my eyes, and healed my heart!

Acknowledgments

Above all others, I'd like to thank my husband for being my knight in shining armor. He has been my best friend and strongest supporter for more than thirty years and has introduced me to the true meaning of unconditional love. Thank you, Honey, for believing in me and encouraging me through every aspect of this book, my biggest endeavor yet!

To my two sons, Troy and Rod, who have taught me much about motherhood and the many reasons for executing unconditional love, thank you and I love you guys!

As a single mom in the fifties, it was very hard to work fulltime and raise two small children. With no child support to speak of, my mother managed to make enough money for the three of us to live comfortably. To my mother, I simply say, Thank you, Mom, for all of your love, advice, and life lessons that you taught me; I love you more than you'll ever know.

To my other best friend, Mark Evans, for teaching me about patience, I say, Thank you! You are the most tolerant person I have ever met. Thanks for putting up with me for over twenty-five years and for being instrumental in the writing of this book.

To my father, Vito, for all of his inspiration, guidance, and loving advice, I say, Thank you from the bottom of my heart! For always being there for me when I needed someone to talk to, I am eternally grateful. I admire you for your incredible humbleness and spirituality.

To my good friends, Ron and Raine Schulte, for their constant companionship, advice, and high energy, I say, Thank you for really coloring my life in so many ways. It is hard to know where my thoughts end and yours begin because we are connected on so many levels.

To my three oldest grandchildren, Hunter, Maria, and Timothy, I say, A big Thank You! Your enthusiasm for life and the love that you exude are the greatest gifts that anyone could receive. You guys are fun, exciting, and a pure delight to be around. I'll never get enough of you. Grandma loves you a whole bunch! As Timmy once put it, ìGrandma, I love you never-ending!î I'm going to hold you to that, little man.

Someone that I could never leave out is my good friend, Jean Walters. Jean, you were instrumental in pointing Mark and me in the right direction spiritually. You are a wonderful teacher, counselor, and friend. For all that you are and all that you stand for, I thank you wholeheartedly.

Finally, I would like to say to all of the psychics, mediums, and counselors of the quaint little town of Cassadaga, Florida: Thank you, thank you, thank you! I never get enough of what Cassadaga has to offer. As a spiritual community, it is a place I constantly want to visit. I always come away feeling spiritually charged and ready to face the world with all of its challenges. I recommend Cassadaga, Florida, to anyone who needs to get away and recharge!

⊂⊗ Table of Contents ⊗⊃

 Prefix

By Linda Yust

It has become obvious to the most casual observer that the interest in the supernatural and (or) paranormal has risen tremendously over the last few years. Television alone has promoted these phenomena with shows, such as *Ghost Whisperer*, *The Medium*, *Supernatural*, *Heroes*, *Cross Roads*, and now *Phenomenon* (not to mention the volume of metaphysical books flying off the bookshelves in the past decade). It is no secret that people are very much interested in the world of the unknown these days. They are more curious now than they have ever been about the unexplainable occurrences that happen around them. However, it seems that most people do not know what to make of these strange little circumstances, so they simply ignore them.

Although I am not a celebrity or a well-known personality, I do think that I can reach millions of people who are looking for the answer to the question, "What just happened?" (in spite of the fact that I am unknown). I do, however, commend all of the wonderful celebrities and high-profile individuals, who add credibility to this arena of life, because it makes them real people instead of a persona. To all of the celebrities that have appeared on the shows of John Edward (*Crossing Over* and now *Cross Roads*), Larry King, Montell Williams, Oprah, and many other programs, I say to you, Way to go! You guys put yourselves in a very vulnerable place to help raise universal consciousness, and for that, you should be commended.

In my book, *Did That Just Happen?*, I report strange phenomena that happened to me in story after story, and in two chapters, I record what goes on in a séance; additionally, one chapter is dedicated to a past life regression. I include pictures of my family (mostly deceased loved ones) for the purpose of putting a face with each story in hopes of adding credibility as well as out of respect for my loved ones.

It's true that there is an abundance of books out there on the subject, and I probably own most of them. So, why would I attempt to write a book about the paranormal/supernatural?

For starters, I find it most amazing that we can communicate with our loved ones who have passed over to the other side. It is quite a healing experience to know that they did not leave us and are still very much aware of what goes on in our lives. Second, I find it astonishing that a great number of people find it difficult to talk openly about their experiences. I can't tell you the number of times that I have spoken to someone about one of my experiences, and they have responded with "Well, I've never told anyone, but this is what happened to me." Still, there are those who believe that nothing like this ever happens to them. So, while the general public is fascinated by all of the supernatural and (or) paranormal occurrences, they somehow do not or cannot relate to it in their own lives ...

I do not recall being open to this psychic ability as a child, and I can't really tell you when it first began; to me, that is not important. What is important is that everyone should know that they have this ability, whether they recognize it or not. Most of the time the word *coincidence* is used way too often, and people miss out on the "signs" or the "messages" that are meant for them. When you think about it, people everywhere ignore messages from their loved ones without even realizing it. How sad that is for the spirit who really has something important to say.

I love to watch people's faces light up when I talk about some of the wonderful paranormal events that take place in my life and listen as they exclaim how they are going to pay closer attention to the next "weird thing" that happens to them. What an incredible connection we have with each other and with the massive universe that surrounds us, if we would only take advantage of the gifts that God gave us.

I believe that the simplicity of my own story can help millions of people acknowledge and receive the signs and messages that are all around them. Healing messages are long overdo and are needed to "jump start" our loving connection to each other as well as to the worlds beyond.

Foreword

By Jean Walters, DM, DD, CRT

I have known Linda Yust for many years. She is what I call "a Seeker," which simply means she looks for truth everywhere she goes and more often than not, she finds it. She is a woman with an open heart and generous spirit. Her desire to share her insight with the world comes through clearly in "Did that Just Happen?" Her book sets forth the vision and desire that each reader realize that living in the world does not necessitate being of the world, that we are spiritual beings, and can embrace that reality.

As Doctors Albert Einstein, David Hawkins, Steven Hawkin, John Hagelin, Fred Alan Wolf and many other great scientists have attested, we live in a world of energy. Linda shows in her manuscript that this world of energy is not just a physical realm, but spiritual as well. Her stories help people validate their own experiences and realize there is much more to life than meets the eye and perhaps helps others accept and, in deed, rejoice in their spiritual self.

As we grow in sensitivity and accept "supernatural" events, we find that they are as natural as breathing air. Soon, we begin to understand, as Linda has, that we are all connected, we are all guided, and we are all loved.

Jean Walters, DM, DD, CRT
Personal Growth Consultant

 # Foreword

By Victor P. Vogenitz
Certified Medium, Healer and Teacher

It is my pleasure and honor to have been ask to write the forward for this book. In all the 40 years of my study and work as a medium specializing in Physical Phenomena, I have never met a group of people with such wonderful energy as Mark, Linda, Ron, and Raine.

I know that a first time reader of such events might find it hard to understand how such active events as the two seance's in this book could have taken place, but trust us they did and more.

Some would ask how can such active events take place with a group that was new to Seance? The answers are simple:

1. They are good friends who's energies have work together in light and love for many years.

2. These events took place at the Seance Room, in the Colby Temple in Cassadaga Florida. This room is referred to as "The Heart" of our temple and the center for energy in our camp. Since it's dedication in 1923, thousands of Seance's have been held in this room by some of the Finest mediums in modern Spiritualism. I myself alone have held as may as one hundred Seance's in a year in this room. The residual energy alone is incredible. The spirits of all the wonderful mediums who have passed over in the history of Cassadaga are always willing to help assist those who attempt to communicate with the other side.

3. The Medium. Forty years ago at sixteen years of age, I started studying Physical Phenomena Mediumship in Cassadaga. My family was filled with it's share of naturally talented people. Mediumship, the metaphysical, psychic events, things of this nature were never treated as unusual or spooky. If it was a "Gift"it is was one that I had to work hard to hone and polish.

4. Spirit I know that all of us were drawn together by the hand of Spirit for a purpose. It was if I were meeting old friends that I had lost contact with when I met them for the very first time. We were placed here together in this space and time to begin a very special journey together.

I look forward with great anticipation to the time they return to Cassadaga and our Seance table. In the mean time I enjoy our communications by E-mail, the updates of events taking place in their lives, and the love they have to share.

As words come short of describing the real nature of events in our Seance's, they too come short in describing what a truly wonderful experience it has been for me, sharing my life with them.

Mr. Victor P. Vogenitz
Certified Medium, Healer, and Teacher.

1

I Forgot To Do My Homework

——— 1967 ———

The year was 1967, and I was a senior in high school. During one of my classes, a rather odd thing happened to me. My last class of the day was English, and I was lucky enough to share that hour with my best friend, Donna. We always had a lot going on in our teenage lives. It's hard to believe, I know. But we spent countless hours at school and away from school, double dating and spending summer vacations together, mostly at the Lake of the Ozarks in southern Missouri. Anyway, back to English class...

On this particular Friday, we had been given an assignment to compile a five-minute speech that we would give in front of the class at the beginning of the following week. Well, with the weekend ahead of us, we thought of nothing but our plans for the following two days. So, just like any other high school senior, we "partied" our brains out. So much to do in so little time!

Fast-forwarding to sixth hour English class the following Monday, I sat in the last desk of the first row of seats; my friend Donna sat in front of me. I was already in my seat when Donna came in and sat down, spinning around to talk before the teacher came in as usual.

"So," she said, "what is your speech about?"

My eyes grew to the size of large saucers. "What speech? Oh my gosh! #@%*"+%#! I totally forgot to do my homework!" I yelped.

Her sympathetic response did little to calm my nerves. "Well, don't worry too much about it. Mr. Gauvin has a lot of students to get through in an hour, so maybe he won't get to you today."

With thirty-five students in the classroom, I prayed Donna was right. Even though I was an A student (in English anyway), this was a big part of our final grade. The bell rang, everyone found their seats, and the teacher stood at the front of the classroom. He picked up his stack of papers and headed to the back of the room, where he expected to listen to our speeches. Big oops! He sat down right behind me. *Now, what are the chances of that happening?* I thought. Not even a moment later, he called on the first student to give his speech, sparing no time in getting started. *Why is he in such a big hurry? We have a whole hour, after all.*

The first student gave his speech, and it was over in a fraction of a second, then we were on to our second victim—I mean, student. The second student finished his speech just as rapidly. As student after student completed their speeches, time began to blur. *Why are they going so fast? Isn't five minutes longer than that? We have a whole hour; slow down, people!*

The teacher called the next student to give a speech and ... wait ... *did I just hear my name called?* No, I was probably being paranoid. *He couldn't have just called my name. Linda, get a hold of yourself, girl.* Oh, but the second time he announced the name it was definitely mine. *Now what do I do?* I slowly stood up and started my long walk toward the front of the classroom, and as I did Donna looked up at me and said, "What are you doing?"

I didn't answer her because—well—I did not know what I was doing. I walked to the front of the classroom in a daze. I didn't remember getting out of my seat or even passing my fellow students on my way through the rows of desks. *What is happening to me? Am I having an out- of-body experience?* My body was not under my control; it felt eerie and strange. When I reached the front of the room, I turned around to face the class, opened my mouth to speak, and from my lips came a stupid joke that I heard years ago when I was a child. The joke had to be told mimicking a strange nasal sound so as to imply that the boy, the character in the joke, had a speech impediment.

I found myself saying, "There was this young guy who had a hard time making friends, so he wasn't very popular because of the way he spoke (he talked funny). He could not get any dates; girls just didn't want to go out with him. However, after some time, this one girl felt really sorry for him; so hoping to raise his morale, she decided to go out with him. When the date was about over, the young man didn't quite know what he should do. Would a good-bye kiss be out of the question? Of course, it was; how awkward would that be? So he opted to just walk her up to her door and say goodnight. And that is just what he did, but as he turned to walk away, the girl called out to him, 'Wait.' He turned back around to see what she wanted. Looking at him compassionately, she handed him a Kleenex and asked him to blow his nose. He took the tissue from her and loudly blew his nose." (Here, I covered my mouth and nose and imitated a fog horn before continuing.) "Afterwards he said, 'Thanks,' with a clear sounding voice," I finished.

Now, for the life of me, I do not know how or even why I remembered that joke. If I had been conscious instead of comatose, I probably wouldn't have told it at all. So, there had to be divine involvement.

The class roared with laughter and even applauded me. I was in shock to say the least. Still standing in front of the classroom, I looked to my left through a window in the closed door and saw the kids in the classroom across the hall leaning over the front of their desks, peering into our classroom, and trying to see what all of the commotion was about. I walked back to my seat; kids still clapped, while I sat down and tried to digest what just happened. Confused and somewhat stunned, I sat there as Donna turned around smiling at me and whispered, "You had me believing that you forgot to do your homework!"

She seemed a little perturbed with me. But as I sat there dumbfounded, trying to make sense out of it, I came to the conclusion that something or someone had just taken over my mind, body, and—oh yeah—spirit. Much to my delight, I remained an A student in English!

Years later, I realized the significance of this story. I failed to do my homework, but my guides did not fail me. I am quite pleased that they saved me from a poor grade and an embarrassing moment. It is good to know that someone up there is looking out for me, and my guide certainly has a sense of humor, no doubt.

So, if you find yourself moving around or apparently speaking on autopilot, you may not want to react as flippantly as I did. It may be your guardian angels working overtime on your behalf. We don't always know who or what is helping us, so consider whispering a grateful thank you before moving on.

My best friend Donna Greishabor and I in 1967

2

Hand on My Shoulder

1985

M y beloved grandmother passed away when I was sixteen years old; it very much impacted me because of our closeness. I loved her dearly, and at sixteen, I didn't possess the capacity to grasp what happens to us when we die. With much going on in my life at that time, dealing with the loss was particularly difficult for me. I do not recall having any type of other-worldly contact with my grandmother until I was around thirty-seven years old.

We lived in a fairly new house in a suburb of St. Louis when my grandmother visited me. I stood at the kitchen sink, doing dishes and gazing out the widow into the courtyard. Suddenly, I felt the weight of a hand on my right shoulder. I slowly turned around, expecting to see my husband Mark or my older son Troy; I forgot that at that time of day, Mark was at work and Troy was at school. When I twisted around, I saw no one. While turning back to face the sink, my grandma came to mind. Feeling faint, my knees buckled. But as I started to slide to the floor, I caught myself on the edge of the sink. The soles of my feet burned, and a strange sensation rose up in my body, which frightened me.   But then I heard my grandmother compassionately say, "I love you."

Once I realized what happened, so many emotions surged inside of me, and I hardly could contain my excitement. This wonderful experience remained with me all of these years. At the age of fifty-seven, it still feels like it happened only yesterday!

If you have found yourself in a similar circumstance, then you know the feeling of *euphoria* that I reference. I strongly believe that the burning sensation I felt travel through my body was actually a sort of "healing" given to me by my grandmother—a transfer of unconditional love.   Instead of fearing the unknown, search for the answers to your unexplainable, paranormal incidents. Talk about them to your friends or loved ones. You might be surprised to discover that you are not alone in these experiences.

My grandmother, Alma Rebecca Lassen, in the 1960's

3

Apparition in the Cemetery

──────── September 1991 ────────

My best friend, Mark Evans, took me out to dinner for my forty-second birthday on September 22, 1991, a Friday evening; the next night, he accompanied me to a Michael Bolton concert on Saturday evening. My husband, Mark, had traveled to Phoenix, Arizona, because of his mother's ill health. Evans picked me up around 6:00 p.m. on Friday, and we went to Tony Romas, a nearby restaurant. Tony Viviano, the entertainer, handed out red carnations to all of the ladies present. When I returned home after dinner, I placed the carnation in a vase and set it on one of the end tables in the living room.

On Saturday evening, Evans picked me up in his corvette, and we started down Manchester Road on our way to the concert. It started to drizzle, and as we passed Holy Cross Cemetery, I spotted a young woman standing over a burial site. Something appeared very odd; no car was parked in the cemetery. A dense wooded area, not close to any homes, surrounded the cemetery. And yet, in the sprinkling rain, this woman stood in the middle of the cemetery. Something else seemed slightly weird; through the light rain from about 200 yards away, I clearly could see that the woman had shoulder-length blond hair. She wore a white blouse, blue slacks, and white tennis shoes; she stood—maybe even hovered—slightly above the grass. The whole scene puzzled me.

After driving a few hundred feet past the cemetery, Evans decided to turn around and go back to his house to exchange his corvette for his truck. As we passed the cemetery for the second time, only a few seconds later, I saw that the woman had vanished.

Where did she go? No car came out of the cemetery, and no one ran or walked in either direction. *How did she disappear so fast?* I knew that I would have to investigate this at a later date.

On Monday morning, I dressed for the office—a little earlier than normal—because I wanted to visit Holy Cross Cemetery. I thought that if I could pinpoint the spot where the young woman stood when I saw her, I might be able to figure out who she was or whom she was visiting. I am not sure why I felt compelled to find this out, but I knew from past experiences that something or someone drew this to my attention. I first thought that maybe this young woman recently lost a child and was there visiting. On my way out, as I walked through the living room, I spotted the red carnation that I placed in the vase on Friday night.

I am going to a cemetery; I may as well take the flower with me and place it on the grave.

When I arrived at the small cemetery, I parked my car and walked to where I remembered seeing the woman. I proceeded to look for a recent burial (a spot where the soil would still be fresh or piled in a mound) around the suspected area. I couldn't find what I was looking for, so I broadened my search by including a row on either side of where I stood. As soon as I did, I spotted a fresh mound of dirt and marched over to it. I recognized instantly that I stood exactly where the woman had stood; when I looked down at the grave, I saw a red carnation lying on the ground—just like the one I held in my hand.

I do not believe in coincidences, not after all of the wonderful experiences I have faced. No headstone or markings of any kind identified the person buried there, just the red carnation. So, I began talking to the soul whose lifeless body lay just beneath the soil. "I do not know you, nor do I know why I am here, but I will pray for your soul, and that you are in a better place and at peace," I said softly and reverently. Then, I laid the red carnation on the ground next to the other one and walked back to my car. As I left the cemetery and drove out of the main gate, I heard the words, "Thank you," and though there was no gender to the voice, I somehow knew that the voice came from the grave occupant.

I never discovered who the woman was or even who was buried there, but I did receive a type of spiritual healing that day. I repeated my story to several people who I knew would understand and appreciate my experience. But it was only when I relayed the story to my mom and aunt that I realized there was more to the story than I originally thought.

I visited my mom at her home in St. Charles, and my aunt

just happened to be there. I started telling them what occurred at the cemetery a few days earlier. As I described the young woman in the cemetery and her clothing, I stopped abruptly. I realized that I was wearing a white blouse, blue pants, and white tennis shoes, and I had shoulder-length blond hair. *What is going on?* My mom looked at me and said nothing; my aunt looked at me like I had three heads, and I wondered if maybe she wasn't right! *What else could they think?* My only saving grace was the total look of bewilderment on my face and the fact that they knew me; I don't concoct stories.

I have learned simply to accept what happens and not discredit any of my experiences because they are all gifts from God, even if we do not understand them at the time. I have faith in my spirituality and in the afterlife; I know that life is eternal and that we never die. I never worry about what other people believe or disbelieve; that is their prerogative. I do, however, believe that if I choose not to share my experiences with others, then the experiences will cease to happen. I consider my openness to the other side of a gift from God, and my life has truly been blessed because of it.

Do not second-guess yourself if you happen upon an apparition; they do exist, and if you see them, you most likely were meant to see them. You may not be able to figure out who they are or why they are there, but just accept that you did in fact experience the sighting.

4

Lady's Laughing Voice

——— Fall of 1991 ———

After my mother-in-law, Joyce, died on October 1, 1991, my father-in-law, Larry, was scarcely seen. They owned a huge home in Phoenix, Arizona that he prepared to sell. At that time, Mark and I decided to add a master suite to the lower level of our house, so that Larry would have a place to stay for as long as he needed. Back and forth a lot, much to our dismay, he did not spend much time with us. We thought it best to give him plenty of room to mourn his wife, so that's exactly what we did.

On a Sunday evening in November of 1991, Mark and I sat in our bedroom when Larry came home from his trip to Arizona. It was late, close to bedtime, but Mark said he wanted to go downstairs to say good night to his father. I was reading a book. All of a sudden, I heard a woman's voice laughing with the voices of Mark and his dad in the background. I could not believe what I was hearing; *Larry didn't bring a woman home with him, did he?* I suspected the worse but hoped I was wrong. Now, I was very disturbed to think that I could be right.

When Mark came upstairs, I asked him, "Did your dad bring a woman to our house?"

Mark looked perplexed and answered, "No, why would you ask me that?"

I said suspiciously, "There's no woman downstairs?"

Mark said, "Linda, my dad is the only one downstairs."

Flabbergasted, I knew that I had distinctly heard a woman's voice, laughing and talking with Mark and his dad. Months later, I discovered that the voice I heard was that of Mark's deceased mother.

Years ago, Joyce prompted us to start thinking about life after death. On a trip to Laughlin, Nevada, with Joyce and Larry, she turned around in the front seat of the van and said, "You know, I read that when you die, your spirit hangs around your body for about three days afterwards, not knowing that you have expired." She continued, "You talk to the ones you've left behind, but they can't hear you, so you keep trying to get their attention."

You may be thinking, "How ironic that she is the one to prove that theory to me!" It's not so inconceivable to someone who believes that there are no coincidences. Just think about it, who better to "get their point across" than the person who opened your mind to it in the first place! In my mind, I heard a woman's voice (clairaudience), but I did not distinctly recognize it as being Joyce's voice at the time.

My mother-in-law, Joyce M. Yust

5

Get Up!

1991

My husband Mark and I began recording our dreams because of their constant significance to what was occurring in our lives. Joyce, my deceased mother-in-law, started visiting and making her presence known to me via clairaudience (hearing her voice). And now, she started coming to me in dreams.

Mark and I went to bed as usual around ten o'clock. Around midnight, I felt the urge to use the bathroom but was either too tired to get up just then or just too lazy—I don't know which. Anyway, I kept fighting the urge and tried to return to sleep, which proved to be impossible, since I constantly heard a voice say, "Get up; get up!" in my head. I finally decided to listen to the voice, so that I could go back to sleep. I got up, used the bathroom, and went back to sleep. Around two a.m., I was once again awakened by a voice yelling, "Larry, get up; Larry, get up!"

My father-in-law stayed with us, since the death of his wife. We built another master bedroom in the lower level (as stated in the previous chapter) for him after her death. Initially, Larry's snoring woke me up, and then I heard the voice telling him to get up. I have to say that at the time, I did not recognize the voice as Joyce's voice.

As every other morning, Mark kissed me good-bye as he left for work. However, this morning, he added, "Listen to the tape recorder before you come into work; I taped a dream I had. Don't forget!" I said that I would, rolled over, and went back to sleep. When I got up, I started running my bathwater and noticed the tape recorder on the counter with a note attached: "Listen to my dream!" I turned the recorder on and listened intently as Mark spoke. "Normally, the alarm clock wakes me up at 6:50 a.m., and I get ready for work and leave at seven-thirty. This morning, however, I was awakened at quarter to seven by a voice saying, 'Mark, get up. Its time for work! Mark, get up!'" Well, finally awake, I deciphered what happened. I realized in that moment that it was Joyce, who was trying very hard to get our attention.

I began to pay closer attention, not only to my dreams, but to those inner voices in my head. How wonderful is the reality that from the other side, we can hear our loved one's voices and know that they are still very much aware of what goes on in our lives but most importantly that they are okay!

You should never assume that the voice you hear in your head is your own imagination. As bizarre as that may sound, it's true. One of the ways in which spirit's energies contact you is through your subconscious mind. A spirit can contact you when you are doing something that becomes mechanical, automatic, or mundane, such as doing the dishes. If an idea pops into your head unexpectedly, it may have come from somewhere other than your own mind.

My mother and father-in-law, Joyce and Larry Yust

6

The Gold Christmas Ornament

——Christmas of 1991——

W hen Joyce died, everyone came to our home after the funeral. All of the flower arrangements from the church were delivered to our house, and as everyone left to go home, I invited them to take whatever flowers they wanted.

The first Christmas after Joyce's death was extremely hard on everyone, especially Mark's younger sisters. It was only fitting that all of his sisters wanted to spend the holidays with the family in St. Louis, particularly at our house. Mark's youngest sister lived in New York; his middle sister lived in Arizona, and the oldest of his sisters lived in San Francisco, California. Mark's dad moved in with us for a short time until his house in Arizona sold and he finalized other business. He wasn't around much, but we knew that he was a very private man and one that deserved his space.

I spent many hours preparing the house, getting it ready for my husband's family. I decorated every room, hoping to make it as warm and inviting as possible. I also did much baking and food preparation for more people than we normally have at Christmas time.

I decorate my Christmas tree in such a way that it takes me around three to four days to complete it, but it is well worth the effort. People say that my tree has a majestic aspect to it, so you can sit and gaze at it for hours and simply get lost in its beauty.

As I put the finishing touches on the tree, I started thinking about Joyce. I missed her, and I was angry with Larry because he hadn't been spending much time around us. Anyway, I started talking to Joyce, telling her that if she would have taken better care of herself, she might still be here with us. I finished the top of the tree, climbed down the ladder, and sat in a nearby armchair to view my work. As I sat there distraught, gazing at the finished product, a gold ornament popped off the middle of the tree, hit the floor, and rolled right up to my feet. I was stunned. *How could a glass ornament fly off of the tree like that? Shouldn't it have fallen straight down, caught on a lower limb, or maybe even continued to fall through the limbs to the floor?* It was as though someone flicked it with their finger to send it flying off of the tree. Then a strong sensation engulfed me; this was Joyce. She sent that ornament flying off the tree and rolled it right up to my feet. I knew it was her; there was no doubt in my mind. I looked down at the ornament and said aloud, "Oh, you are here with us. Aren't you, Joyce?" I picked the ornament up and placed it back on the tree, but I decided to place it out on a limb by itself, so that I would be reminded of Joyce's presence every time I looked at the tree and, of course, to show the family, when I relayed the story to them.

After writing this article, I thought it pertinent to include a picture of the Christmas tree from that year. I went through all of my pictures until I found the Christmas pictures of all of the family and the tree. As I located the ornament hanging out on the limb, I was taken back to the time when I placed it there. But it wasn't until I enlarged the 4x6 color picture that I noticed something even more remarkable. I studied the picture trying to figure out why the top portion of the tree looked darker than the rest of the tree. Then I figured that maybe some of the small lights must have burned out. But in the process of studying the tree, I noticed the orange glow to the right of the gold ornament (both are circled). I could see a face in that orange glow; when I copied the picture in black and white, the face was even more predominate.

This was something quite different from the previous experiences that I have had with Joyce. I wasn't "hearing" a voice in my head; this wasn't clairaudience. I distinctly felt her presence; this was clairsentience. In chapter two, I first experienced clairsentience when my grandmother put her hand on my shoulder, and then clairaudience when I heard her say that she loved me.

All of us have experiences like this at some point in our lives. You may be afraid of them or maybe you simply **choose** to forget them. Either way, I feel they are a gift and should be embraced and shared as such because of the "healing" properties they provide. Once you become open to receiving these occurrences, I believe that they begin to happen with more frequency. Remember always to ask for God's protection against any negative energy that may be around and receive only spirit energies that emerge from God's light.

Christmas of 1991, our first Christmas after the death of my mother-in-law, Joyce. The infamous gold ornament hangs out on a limb by itself because that is where I placed it when I returned it to the tree. If you look on the left side of the tree, about two-thirds of the way up, you will see the small gold ornament hanging there. If you look directly to the right of the ornament you will see a face.

Gold Fairy Dust

—Friday, January 15, 1992—

Shortly after my mother-in-law died, I dreamed she came to me. I'm really not sure if I saw myself in a dream or I actually left my body and viewed it lying on the bed. Either way, I lay on my left side when I saw—of all things— gold fairy dust surrounding me from my waist up to my head. I watched as I put my left arm around my body in a hugging fashion and said, "I love you too, Joyce." The next thing I remember is a feeling of being suffocated. I thought someone was in the bedroom trying to smother me with a pillow. I sat up abruptly and started breathing rapidly. Mark woke up and said, "What's wrong?" I explained to him what happened.

Mark and I had been estranged from his family for three years because of something that happened at his sister Mary's wedding. During this time, Joyce was diagnosed with breast cancer. Mark received a call from his dad, informing him of the grim situation.

A very spiritual person and originally Protestant, Joyce became Catholic, but she retained many phobias. We believe it was her fears that caused the cancer. Joyce was a very loving and giving person but extremely opinionated and stuck in her ways. She was convinced that praying to God would save her, but she waited until it was too late, and the cancer was too advanced.

After the call from his dad, Mark decided to visit his mom. The trip to Phoenix went well, and Mark made three more visits after that. On the last visit to Arizona, I went with Mark to see his mother. While there, Mark, his dad, and I stood in the kitchen talking; a very strong feeling of sadness came over me that I could not dismiss.

I said, "I can't take this anymore," and I went into the bedroom to talk to Joyce. I sat down on the chair next to her bed and told her how sorry I was for the problems that arose between us.

She replied, "It's all your fault." At this point, the accusation did not seem to matter. My heart broke that she had to suffer like this. When it was time to leave, I went in to the bedroom again to say good-bye. As I sat on the bed next to her, we hugged; she didn't turn away from me like she usually did when I kissed her on the cheek and said good-bye for the last time. A week later on October 1, she passed.

Ironically, Mark and I took care of the funeral arrangements, I believe, because we were the only ones that lived in St. Louis. After the funeral, everyone congregated at our home.

Little did I know that such a simple gesture of swallowing my pride and opening up my heart could lead to a life-changing experience. Joyce has been with me ever since, and I credit her for some of the most wonderful occurrences that have ever taken place in my life. To me, she exemplifies the true meaning of Unconditional Love.

After further study on astral projection (out-of-body experience), I have come to the conclusion that I did indeed leave my body. The experience I had of being suffocated upon waking is said to be what happens when you return to your physical body. In Harold Sherman's book, *How to Make ESP Work for You*, Mr. Sherman poses a question to Mr. John Mittl of Kempton, Pennsylvania: "In the astral, what appears to be your means of existence? Do you breathe as you do in the physical?" Mr. Mittl responded, "While in the astral body I have a feeling of complete freedom ... As for breathing, I am seldom conscious of doing so on the astral plane. However, when I return to my physical body, I am aware of immediate, heavy, labored breathing, provided I awake upon re-entrance." This definitely explains the feeling of suffocation that I experienced.

I left my body only on one other occasion. I didn't know when it happened. I was told about it later when a friend described how he awoke to see me peering down at him from the corner of his room.

This can happen to you while you sleep or you are in your subconscious mind and strongly thinking about someone or somewhere you long to be. Have you ever had someone say to you, "I saw you at the mall yesterday," or "what were you doing at _____ last night?" Do you remember thinking about going to the mall or thinking about that other location? It is possible, and it does happen; I am living proof!

8

Tell Mark I Love Him

———— January 17, 1993 ————

On a brisk Sunday morning in January, we awoke and started milling around the house. Mark said, "After lunch, why don't we go up to the mall and visit the book store?" Since reading is a favorite past time of mine, I didn't question him as to why he wanted to go; I just agreed before he changed his mind. You see, my husband is not a devoted reader nor is he an avid shopper, and since both of these were my favorite pastimes, I saw no reason to ask why. I just agreed to his request. At lunch, we discussed the dream that I had on Friday night about Joyce coming to me and telepathically telling me that she loved me.

We headed to the bookstore; on the way, I discovered Mark's intent. He wanted to find a book on the afterlife. His mother passed a year and two months ago, and, I guess, he wondered about her. We found three metaphysical books on the subject and one in particular, *We Don't Die*, by Joel Martin and Patricia Romanowski. This book actually protruded off the shelf; it arrested my interest, or maybe I should say that Joyce captured my attention.

Once home, Mark sat down in front of the TV and proceeded to watch a Sunday matinee movie, while I sat on the sofa behind him to read. I had started reading the book about Michael Landon written by his daughter and wanted to finish reading it before I started a new one. Anxious to start reading *We Don't Die*, I rushed through Landon's book. Once I finished reading it, I picked up the new book and started to read first the foreword and then the introduction as I do with all of the books I read. But when I started to read the first chapter, something strange happened.

I heard a voice in my head say, "Tell Mark I love him." I thought it odd that I would think something like that, so I just shook my head and tried to read again. Once more, I heard the voice say, "Tell Mark I love him." This time, I thought silently, *I can't do that; he'll think that I'm crazy!* I heard in response, "Tell him anyway!"

Well, at this point, I decided to do as I was told. I said, "Mark, your mom just told me to tell you she loves you." Now, I don't know how I knew it was Joyce, but when I opened my mouth, that's what came out. Mark turned around to look at me and said, "That's great; tell her I love her too," and he went back to watching his movie. *Okay, that was weird!* Once I delivered the message to Mark, I had no problem continuing to read my new book, *We Don't Die* (excellent reading by the way).

At ten p.m., Mark's movie ended, and he asked me if I was ready for bed. I was, so we headed to the bedroom. But as I started to climb into bed, I remembered the strange message that

I gave Mark from his mother. And I said, "Mark, why didn't you question me when out of the clear blue, I told you that your mother said that she loved you?"

"Because don't you remember the dream that you had Friday night, when my mom telepathically told you that she loved you?"

"Yeah, so?"

His next few words left me incredulous, "When my mom was alive, she never once told me that she loved me, and I just wished that she would have told *me* that she loved me."

"I didn't know that!" *Wow!* It finally dawned on me that this was confirmation that Joyce had indeed been coming to me. Mark said that he never doubted me once.

I said, "Yeah, but how great is it that she used me to tell you she loved you?"

Mark said, "I guess I'm just too dense for her to get through to me."

"No, that's not it at all; she knew that I needed the confirmation, so that I would not second guess myself. It had to happen this way to have the most impact on you, me, and the world!"

This is one of my most treasured experiences for several reasons: my deceased mother-in-law first helped me find the book, *We Don't Die*, and she then recognized her son's need to hear those three little words from her, but more importantly, she used me to deliver that wonderful message. I still feel euphoric every time I think of this story, and it is my deepest desire that everyone reading this will eventually experience this kind of emotion.

It can and does happen to everyone at some point in their lives; the fact that most people are not open to these phenomena may be the reason they miss them. Or maybe they just do not recognize it as anything more than their own thoughts. Either way, it is a true pity to miss something as extraordinary as this when it happens. Even though we consider mediums and psychics to be gifted because of their amazing talents (which by the way they embrace, cultivate, and use day after day), we fall short in recognizing our own gifts. It takes an exceptional person to do what John Edward, James Van Praagh, Allison DuBois, and many, many others do with their lives on a daily basis. I am not suggesting that we can do what they do, but I am proposing that you can expand and develop the gifts that God gave to **you**, simply by opening up to them and accepting them as such!

This picture of Joyce was taken in her backyard in Phoenix, Arizona after her cancer surgery.

9

Rod's Floppy Disc

———— March 15, 1992 ————

While in Oklahoma, my son Rod mailed some of his things home but realized he had sent a floppy disc home by mistake. While talking to him one Sunday, he mentioned that he needed his disc desperately by the following Thursday for a program that he was working on. I told him, "No problem! I'll mail it back to you." For more than six weeks, that disc had laid on the kitchen counter, where no one looked, touched, or even noticed it much. Now that Rod needed it, I couldn't find it anywhere. On several occasions, I searched and searched, turning the house upside down, but I found no sign of his floppy disc.

One morning, as I was getting ready for work, something quite strange happened. As usual, I dressed for the day and went into the bathroom to put on my makeup and style my hair. After that, I decided what shoes to wear. I kept all of my purses in the front bedroom closet because of lack of space in the master bedroom closet. The last thing I do before leaving the house is change purses, so I headed into the front bedroom. As I pulled the matching purse from the overhead shelf, something fell and bounced off my head. *Ouch! What on earth was that!* (Well, it's nice to know that my angels, guardians, deceased relatives—whoever—have a sense of humor). I rubbed my head and looked to the floor only to find the floppy disc laying there. This has happened to me so many times that I have just learned to be very appreciative and always say, "Thank you." I picked up the floppy disc, put it in my purse, and headed to work where I mailed it to Rod.

3

This is my youngest son Rod. This picture was taken in Sept. of 1996 on his wedding day.

෯**10**෯

Distortion Pedal

───── April 10, 1992 ─────

Rod called me from Oklahoma and asked me to send him several items that he wanted and needed, one of which was his distortion pedal that he had sent home two years earlier. Now, I had no idea what a distortion pedal was or what it was used for, only that he described it to me as a little black box. I didn't know where it was, and he couldn't remember where he had left it. I told him that I would search for it and send it when it was found. I began putting all of the items together that he had asked for—all but the distortion pedal. I searched the house for this little black box with no luck finding it.

Meanwhile, I asked my mother (she sews for our business and makes the gambling skirts for our tables) to start stitching identification labels onto the gambling-table skirts to help the guys in the warehouse put the right skirts on the right tables. She said that she would, but she didn't have the labels. I told her that I could bring some to her, since I had plenty of them in my sewing room downstairs.

The next day, I went to my sewing room, which was right next to our storage room. A laundry basket sat on the floor in the storage room, full of ribbons left over from Joyce's funeral. I noticed that one of the ribbons had fallen out of the basket and on to the floor. I walked over to pick up the ribbon. As I bent down to pick it up and return it to the basket, I noticed a black box sitting on one of the storage shelves. Yes, it was Rod's distortion pedal. I could not believe my eyes; I had looked everywhere for that little black box!

In my heart and mind, I know that Joyce was responsible for helping me to locate Rod's distortion pedal. This was just one of the many times that Joyce helped me to locate a lost item.

I have talked with many people who have enlisted the help of angels, deceased relatives, or even guides to help them locate lost items. This is actually a very common occurrence and one that most people feel comfortable with because it doesn't take much effort on their part to simply ask for help. However, how many people actually acknowledge that these entities assisted them, and even more importantly, how many show their gratitude with a simple thank you? Always be courteous, respectful, and, of course, grateful!

My son Rod tooling around in his convertible.

My son Bret wanting to ride his snow mobile.

11

Missing Earrings

1992

M y husband and I own a business with a very big portion of that business being party planning. One of our most successful theme parties is our casino parties. We hire and train our own dealers, and when we do not have enough, we use state dealers. Mark and I both deal. He deals all of the table games and covers as pit boss, and I deal Black Jack. We are hired to do many corporate organizations, celebrity fundraisers, and home parties of all kinds at most of the businesses around town. We are strictly professional and always make sure our dealers dress the part. Our work attire consists of a white tuxedo shirt, black pants, bow tie, and cummerbund.

We had a casino party coming up on the weekend—five days away. I always prepare early by making sure that my shirt, pants, tie, cummerbund, and shoes are all ready to go and in one place. I decided to do the same with my earrings and studs. I went to my jewelry box to gather them and found that they were missing. My favorite earrings (the ones I always wear) were not there! Then I remembered that the last time I dealt, I took off my high heels and earrings on the drive home. I had slipped my earrings down into the toe of my heels, so I wouldn't lose them. *How ironic is that!* I went into my closet, found my black heels, and reached down into the toes—only to come up empty handed. *Now what?* I checked and double-checked the car floorboard but found nothing. I turned my jewelry box upside down and emptied all of the drawers. *They have to be in the house somewhere, but where?* I searched and searched all week long, sometimes twice a day, with the same outcome each time.

Finally, Saturday arrived, the night of the casino party. I dressed and decided that I would have to find another pair of earrings to wear. I went to my jewelry box and opened the top drawer (where I keep all of my good jewelry). In the middle of the top drawer lay my favorite earrings. *Whoa, how can that be? I've looked in this drawer a hundred times. Who put them there? There is no way I missed them; they are in the middle of the drawer in plain sight!* Extremely happy to have found them, I said, "Thank you," to whoever put them there. However, since Joyce has been hanging around and helped me find other lost items, I am almost certain that she was responsible for helping me find my earrings. In my heart, I believe Joyce put the earrings there for me to find. I found my son's floppy disc and distortion pedal, and I'll just bet she was the one who helped me find those items also.

How many times have you located a lost article after searching and searching only to discover it in a place you had looked many, many times? How did it get there, and why didn't you see it the first time? I am sure that skeptics will come up with a million reasons for how this can happen, and that's fine. But for me, I believe that life is eternal and that we are incredible beings while on earth and even more so when we cross over.

My husband Mark and I dressed in our work attire.

12

Last Visit from Joyce

1993

After so many wonderful visits from my mother-in-law, which are all recorded as chapters in this book, it was extremely painful for me for the visits to end. She changed our lives so drastically that I feel a tremendous love and gratitude toward her. While she was still alive, she spoke to us on several occasions about life after death, and I credit her for helping me to find the correct materials to read on the subject. I know that I was guided to all of the books that I purchased because they seemed to jump off the shelves at me. In fact, the first book that I bought, *We Don't Die*, protruded out further than any other book on the shelf.

I have said on several occasions that she taught me the meaning of unconditional love, the most wonderful kind of pure and unassuming love. God gives this kind of love to all of us. As I said, it fully changed my life!

I grew to love her visits and the messages that they revealed. It was remarkable to see and hear her the way she was before the cancer ravished her body. So when she appeared to me on this particular night and told me that this was her last visit, I was devastated. "No," I told her, "don't go, and don't stop coming to me, please!" But she had other business to attend to; you see, life truly is eternal. She must progress as a soul on the other side. As disheartened as I felt, I knew better than to try to hold on to her; it would be wholly selfish of me to do so.

As she appeared to me to say good-bye, she hovered about two and a half feet above the floor. I lay in bed and gazed at the bottom of her long, flowing, red gown with the most brilliant gold emanating out of the long sleeves and the bottom of the hem. She stood perfectly still with her head tilted slightly to one side, looking at me. Breathtakingly beautiful, she smiled sweetly with her hands clasped together in front of her body. She floated above a bright flame of yellow and blue. I watched with an extremely heavy heart as she faded away.

She never came to me in dreams like that again, although my husband and I have felt her presence around us, and she did come to us in the first séance that we had in Casadaga, Florida. At that time, she communicated with Mark and expressed her love to him once again.

A number of people tell me that they have felt a loved one's presence after they passed, and maybe you, dear reader, have also felt the same. There is no one better than you to actually know if the presence you felt was truly that of your loved one. No one can convince you that it didn't happen nor should they be allowed to do so. The presence you felt was a gift from the other side and meant solely for you, so that you might know from the depths of your heart that life truly is **eternal**. In sharing your story with others, you strengthen your faith and give them the gift of hope.

This picture had to be created, because I viewed this scene as I awoke from a sound sleep, and it only lasted a few seconds.

❧13❧

Frankie

——1993——

O n October 12, 1946, my older brother Frankie was born (two years before I came along). Unfortunately, I never knew him because he died at the young age of seven months. I have often thought about him and wondered how my life would have been different if Frankie were here.

I titled this chapter, "Frankie," but after our second séance (chapter 23), I decided to change the title to "Frankie, My Cool Older Brother" because of what Frankie said when he came through. However, when I typed it in the computer and filed it, the document saved as just "Frankie," so I guess that is the most appropriate name for this chapter. Anyone who uses a computer will often tell you that they have a mind of their own, and I wholeheartedly agree. However, I have also heard that spirits manipulate electrical devices, and I witnessed this on several occasions. While I **am** fat fingered many times, this time, I know that I typed it correctly.

Throughout my life, I have thought of Frankie often and wondered about his passing at such a young age. I read many books on the subject of life after death. I tried to figure out if Frankie chose to reincarnate or to stay on the other side. My mother never really talked much about his passing, quite understandably. I remember both of my sons when they were 7 months old like it was only yesterday; I can't imagine the pain of losing either one of them. (My sons are now thirty-seven and thirty-eight years old.) I don't bring up Frankie to my mother any more than necessary out of respect for her feelings.

Nevertheless, my search for knowledge about his whereabouts never waned. Other people may think I am crazy for even considering the possibility of finding an answer to my question. And that's okay because I know in my heart that the answer is out there somewhere, and I will keep pursuing my quest. It *is* just that important to me.

One way I try to find answers, of course, is in prayer. I also write the question down on a piece of paper and put it on the nightstand next to my bed. When I say my prayers, I ask for the answer to be sent to me in a dream, and I also pray that I will remember the dream! This has worked for me on many occasions, and I must say that it is important to know how to interrupt the dream. You cannot accept the dream in a literal sense as dream symbols are involved. With many published books on dreams, if you care to pursue the subject, one of my favorites is *Mary Summer Rain on Dreams*. Another approach would be to consult a reputable psychic or a medium. This has also worked for me, although I seem to be able to interpret most of my dreams on my own after practicing doing so for such a long time.

Frankie did come to me, although I didn't recognize him as Frankie when it happened. I went to bed one evening and asked in my prayers, "Whatever happened to Frankie?" However, I didn't receive my answer until sometime later. When it takes longer than a day, a month, or even a year or two, we may forget about our request or simply give up trying. That is exactly what happened in my case, but God never forgot; He answered my prayers—just not in my time frame. Years later, I received my answer!

I wouldn't say that Frankie came to me in a dream because I was awake when I saw him just as when I saw Joyce. For whatever reason, I awoke from a sound sleep to see a young man in his twenties, standing beside my bed looking down at me. At first, I was startled, thinking that someone had come into my bedroom; when he saw that he startled me, he vanished, but not before I looked at him. He wore a black and ivory, varsity-athlete's jacket and a gold graduation ring. He stood with his arms folded and his chin resting on his fist like Jack Benny. Although I don't remember the color of his hair, it was in the traditional, fifties, James Dean style. I do not recall his face or if I even glanced at his face.

For years, I attempted to decipher who the spirit was but never discovered the answer until our second séance at Cassadaga in 2007—fourteen years later! When Frankie came through during the séance (also known as table tipping), I could not believe it. After all the years of wondering about him, I finally could communicate with him and learn of his location.

When you think that God does not answer your prayers, you may want to reconsider! In *The Secret*, Lisa Nichols states,

"Thank God that there is a time delay ... the element of time delay serves you." This is so true because had this happened to me in a different place and time, I may have not been able to deal with it, nor would I have known how to process it. Everything happens when and how it is suppose to for a very good reason. Keep the faith!

This is baby Frankie, as he sat on my Aunt Bea's front porch. He was just seven months old when he passed on May 14, 1947.

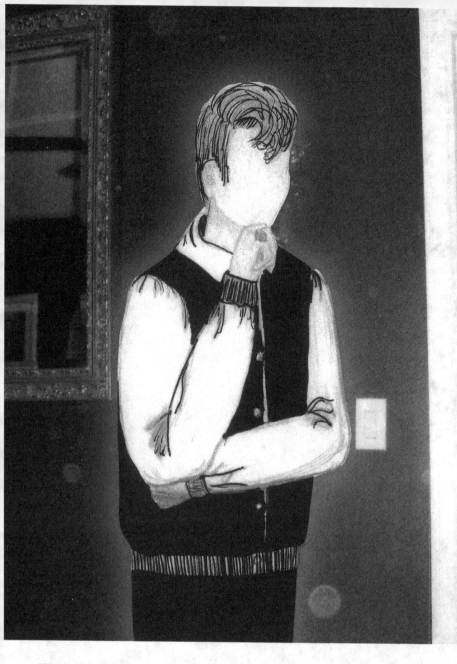

This picture had to be created just like the one in chapter 12, because it is also a vision of a spirit that appeared to me while I was asleep. The apparition was standing by my bed when I awoke, just as you see it. The white round circles on the wall behind him are spirit orbs.

14

Twin Spirits

——————May 1, 1996——————

Early in the morning, I rolled over on my right side and cuddled close to Mark. I looked on the wall as something strange captured my attention. High on the wall and close together, two circular lights (orbs) traveled very fast across the room. At first, I merely thought that they were car lights, but as I closed my eyes to return to sleep, I realized they could not possibly be car lights. We keep our bedroom completely dark to enhance our sleep with darkening shades on the windows with draperies on top. Even though a street runs behind our house, it is much lower than our second-story bedroom, in addition to being on the other side of the creek and behind the density of the trees. After realizing that I had seen two spirits in the form of orbs, I found it hard to go back to sleep. I lay there trying to figure out who the spirits were and the purpose of their visit.

Later on in the summer of the same year, my son Troy and his wife Christine found out that they were having twins. In reflection, I thought that maybe the orbs could have been the spirits of the twins. I have read that while we are still in the spirit world, we have the option to reincarnate back to earth, where we can choose our life situations and even the families that we want to be born into—a wild idea but maybe not so far fetched.

The twins were born on June 6, 1996 and are eleven months older than my youngest grandson, Timmy who was born on April 30, 1997.

When Timmy was two years old, he was playing in the toy room downstairs. He was spending the weekend with us, as he often did. I was in the downstairs kitchen working. All of a sudden, Timmy came running out of the toy room shouting, "Maw-Maw, Maw-Maw!" He ran straight to me and said, "Up, up!!"

The poor little guy's body shook, and he obviously was very scared, so I picked him up in my arms and said, "What's wrong, Tim Tim?"

He said, "Car yights [lights]!" and indicated that there was a car in the toy room. There are no windows in the toy room because it is in the underground portion of our walkout basement between the downstairs bedroom and my sewing room. I knew it could not have been car lights, but I didn't put much thought into it at the time. I merely cuddled Timmy and went into the toy room with him to watch him as he played.

Fast forwarding to 2007—eight years later—I realized that the lights Timmy saw were the same spirit orbs that I saw in my bedroom in 1996. Why it took me so long to figure out, I don't know, but sometimes, things just do not come to you as fast as you think they should. When the same twin orbs appeared to me again in my bedroom in 2007, I began to wonder more about their meaning.

I awoke out of a sound sleep, lying on my left side. I opened my eyes to see two orbs hovering in midair about three feet from my face. They were together just as before; only this time, something else was added to the scene. Off in the distance to the left of the orbs was an old ship, similar to Columbus' Nina, Pinta, and Santa Maria. Since I actively researched my family tree, I immediately attributed the ship to be part of that phenomenon. Recently, I had been finding information about my great-great-grandfather, Emil Lassen, who came to the United States from Copenhagen, Denmark by way of ship. The records say that he crashed his ship into the California coastline in the early 1800s. Why I saw a picture of a ship from that period with the two orbs, I am not quite sure. Later that same night, I awoke for a second time and saw the same two orbs hovering above my husband's head as he lay sleeping.

I have yet to figure out the mystery surrounding the two orbs, but what I do know is that they are around for a reason. I know that the two orbs that I saw (first in May of 1996) are the same orbs that frightened my two-year-old grandson, while he innocently played in his toy room in 1999 and are the same orbs that appeared to me one night in 2007. I can only hope to solve this mystery one day—however long it takes.

You can capture orb energies on a digital camera simply by focusing and snapping. I like to take pictures either at night or against a dark background as they tend to show up clearer.

Rarely do you see them with the naked eye, but if you do, consider yourself fortunate.

When you experience strange phenomena, such as the twin orb sightings, I believe that it is important to document them by recording them in a journal. Even though you may never forget them, you may not remember every important detail surrounding the event. One day you just might want to write a book about them!

This is Hunter, my grandson, taken at Christmas of 1999.
He was three years old when this picture was taken.

This is Hunter's twin sister, Maria.

This is my youngest grandson, Timmy, who is my little
protégé and the spitting image of his father, Rod. Timmy
was two years old when this picture was made.

15

Negative Energy in the Bedroom

——— June 24, 1997 ———

When Mark began snoring very badly, he started sleeping in the front bedroom. Because I wasn't getting any sleep, I remained in the master bedroom. My mom and I argued recently over me continuing to see and talk to my step-dad—after she had broken up with him for the third time. Married and divorced twice, they reconciled just long enough for her to destroy a new relationship that he had just begun. When she dumped him for the third time, I told her that I was having lunch with him on Tuesday of next week. Furiously, she said I was stabbing her in the back by continuing to see or talk to him. I tried to explain to her that he had been the only dad that I had ever known, and he had always been there for me when I needed him. She told me that she did not care; if I wanted to have him in my family, then he would be my only family. She set her mind on destroying all of my family ties, which she accomplished fairly well, because she was furious with me. How my mother gets away with the things she does, I do not know. I guess people, who believe her stories, are just naïve or ready to believe the worst of me. Either way, it's a losing battle and one that I prefer to leave alone because it is my belief that misery loves company.

Because of conflicting schedules, I rescheduled my lunch date with my step-dad for Wednesday. Since my mother was not talking to me, I didn't see any reason to tell her about the change. On Tuesday evening, I went to bed at around ten p.m. I lay on my stomach with both forearms tucked under my pillow; a thin sheet covered me. I was just about to fall asleep, when I felt the covers lift up in the air and then come back down on top of me. I could feel the sheet settle over me as the air swooshed out away from my body. All of a sudden, I felt someone sit down on top of my legs. I turned my head to look behind me only to realize that I was pinned down by no one but paralyzed just the same. Since I had been having visitations from Joyce, I assumed it was she. I asked, "Joyce, is that you?"

But as soon as the words were out of my mouth, I knew it was not her. Her energy was always light and positive; this energy felt determinedly negative and heavy. Suddenly, an electrical shock radiated from my left calve and then again on my right forearm. The feeling was similar to hitting your crazy bone. This scared the *bejeebies* out of me because I have never experienced this type of energy before. Previously being paralyzed, I now knew that this was not the time to be alone, so I jolted out of bed and ran into the front bedroom where Mark slept. I stood beside the bed. *I can't wake him; what will I tell him?* But Mark awoke saying, "What's wrong?"

I simply said, "Can I sleep in here with you?" He held up the covers, and I climbed in next to him. He put his arms around me, which allowed me to feel just how badly I was shaking. After about thirty minutes, his snoring got to me, and I said, "I can't sleep in here; I'll have to go back to our bedroom."

He replied, "Do you want me to go with you?"

I did not hesitate to answer yes. We both went back to the master bedroom, and finally, I fell into a deep slumber. I did not find out until the next day that Mark did not spend the whole night with me. He told me that after I fell asleep, he went back to the front bedroom. Why? He explained that he did not know what was in that room, but the negative energy was so bad he couldn't stay.

About three days later, a Friday, I woke abruptly at 4:38 a.m. out of a sound sleep because a light bulb went off in my head. Something or someone told me that the negative energy that I felt on Tuesday was none other than my own mother!

For whatever reason, my mother always thinks that everyone says or does things to hurt her, a very self-centered notion. She doesn't realize that other people have their own agendas, and they are not always thinking of her when they make decisions in their lives. Whether she is self-centered, immature, uneducated, or all of the above, I am not really sure, but she has acted this way all of my life. Unfortunately, she is the most vengeful person I know, and she will spend the rest of her life getting even, if she thinks someone has wronged her. It makes perfect sense to me that my mother would send negative energy my way, knowing how furious she was with me when she felt that I had gone against her wishes.

Whether negative energy comes from the physical or the astral plane, it is still bad energy, and you want to avoid it as much as possible. Surrounding yourself with God's white light and praying for protection is how I prepare myself when dealing with the paranormal. There are times when you do not see it coming, such as in this story of my mother's revenge. It is very sad but true that I have had to distance myself from my mother and other unhealthy relationships because I am not a masochist, and it does not serve my purpose to remain close to controlling individuals. I am on a spiritual path not one of self-destruction!

In the summer of 1996 this picture was taken of my mom, Laveta LaRosa, on our patio.

❦16❧

Appreciation for a Job Well Done

————March of 1999————

E vans and I were traveling home from Hilton Head, South Carolina, after a week's vacation. I decided to drive my Mercedes 500SL convertible to get some sun along the way. As we drove along the highway listening to CDs, we discussed which restaurant to stop at for lunch. As always, his first choice was Taco Bell. I never really cared where we ate because I like just about everything when it comes to food. Somewhere on the interstate between Tennessee and Georgia, I spotted a Taco Bell and pulled into the parking lot.

We walked into the fast food restaurant and up to the counter to order our food. As I approached the young man behind the counter, he greeted me, "Hello, ma'am, welcome to Taco Bell. May I take your order?" What a pleasant surprise to be greeted with such enthusiasm and warmth and in a fast-food restaurant no doubt! I placed my order and then heard, "Thank you, ma'am, for choosing Taco Bell. Have a nice day!" Mark stood behind me and received the same courtesy from the young man. We picked up our food and sat down at a table to eat our lunch. As we sat there in disbelief, we witnessed this behavior continue as other customers filed in for lunch.

I commented to Mark at how much this young guy resembled one of our employees at work, and he stated that he wished that our employees had just half as much patience and enthusiasm as this guy. We continued to watch and listen as this young man worked and at how the costumers responded to his courteous behavior. Some of them were as pleasantly surprised as we were, while others joked and poked fun at him. I felt amazed at the lack of respect that some of the people showed for this young man—and for themselves. This prompted me to think about how grateful I would be as an employer to have my employees act in this manner, and how grateful I was to be treated with appreciation.

I looked at Mark as he sat across from me enthusiastically eating his burrito; I said, "I am going to show my appreciation to this young man for the manner in which he is doing his job." I reached down to the floor for my purse and took out my wallet.

Mark looked up from his food with his cheeks ballooned out like a chipmunk and said, "What are you going to do?"

I replied, "I am going to go and give him a tip to show my appreciation for a job well done!" I took a hundred-dollar bill out of my wallet.

As I did, Mark's eyes grew as large as two, half-dollar bills. He questioned incredulously, "You're going to give him that hundred-dollar bill?"

Ignoring him, I walked to the front of the restaurant. On my way, I noticed that there was a different person standing behind the counter. I asked him where the young man was that was there a few minutes ago.

He said, "He took a break. Is something wrong?"

I replied, "No, I just wanted to talk to him."

He told me that the other young man was in the back and that he would go to get him. As he walked across to the other end of the room, I followed him to that side of the restaurant and looked back to see several guys taking a break in a small room. The young man came up to me and said, "Yes, ma'am, is everything o.k.?"

I remarked politely, "Oh yes, everything is just fine; I just wanted to tell you how impressed I am with your performance. My husband and I own a company back in St. Louis with quite a few employees, and we would love for our employees to respond as well as you do on the job."

"Why thank you, ma'am," he replied.

I then asked him how many people worked there.

He spun around and looked into the back room to count the people working before turning back to me and saying, "Five, there are five of us working today."

As I placed the hundred-dollar bill in his hand, I told him that I wanted him to share this with his co-workers along with his work ethics. Astonished and gleeful, he shook my hand and said, "Ma'am, I am working my way through college, studying to be a tailor, and if you ever come by this way again, you come over to the college, and I will hem a skirt, a pair of pants—anything you want for free."

I was amazed once again as I silently thought about him going to school for something that I do myself and have taken for granted for so long. I come by it naturally; sewing is something that my mother has been employed to do for over sixty years. All of my relatives sew, and my father worked as a tailor when he was younger.

I thanked him again and told him that I might just take him up on the offer. As I walked back to my table, he sauntered into the back and shared his good fortune with his comrades (and, hopefully, his good work habits too)!

As Mark and I left the restaurant, I asked him if he wouldn't mind driving, so that I could rest my eyes awhile. He obliged and climbed behind the wheel as I crawled into the passenger's seat and closed my eyes.

A few miles down the highway, I turned to look at Mark as he said, "Are you awake? You've got to listen to this song." I told him that I awakened just as the song came on the radio and had heard it from the beginning. The brand new release from Clay Walker was entitled "Chain of Love." This was the first time that we had listened to the song. Strangely, the story of the song goes like this:

> "He was driving home one evening in
> his beat up Pontiac When an old lady flagged
> him down her <u>Mercedes</u> had a flat. He could
> see that she was frightened standing out there

in the snow Till he said I'm here to help you ma'am by the way my name is Joe.

She said I'm from St. Louis and I'm only passing through I must've seen a hundred cars go by this is awful nice of you. When he changed the tire and closed the trunk and was about to drive away, she said how much do I owe you, here's what he had to say.

(Chorus)

You don't owe me a thing I've been there too; someone once helped me out just the way I'm help'n you. If you really want to pay me back here's what you do. Don't let the chain of love end with you.

Well a few miles down the road the lady saw a small cafe she went in to grab a bite to eat and then be on her way. But she couldn't help but notice how the waitress smiled so sweet and she must've been eight months along and dead on her feet. And though she did not know her story and probably never will When the waitress went to get her change from a hundred dollar bill The lady slipped right out the door and on a napkin left a note There were tears in the waitress's eyes when she read what she wrote.

(Chorus)

You don't owe me a thing I've been there too; someone once helped me out just the way I'm help'n you. If you really want to pay me back here's what you do. Don't let the chain of love end with you.

That night when she got home from work the waitress climbed into bed she was thinking about the money and what the lady's note had said As her husband laid there sleeping she whispered soft and low everything is gonna be alright I love you, <u>Joe</u>."

Now you can imagine how peculiar I felt when the song finished playing. With all of the obvious similarities (I underlined them in the song), there is still one that is not quite as obvious. As I mentioned before, my father was a tailor just as the young man in Taco Bell, but what I didn't say was that my father's name was Joe—Joe L. Hawkins.

I cannot explain how such extraordinary phenomenon happens; I only know that it does and that it continues to happen to me to this day. I believe it is my duty to pass along all of the wonderful and weird things that happen in my life, so that others may be able to relate and possibly understand that they are not alone. I also want to thank all of the amazing artists out there like Clay Walker, who tell such wonderful and meaningful stories in their songs. It's not fiction; it really is about life.

Oh, and don't forget: Don't let the chain of love end with you! Thanks, Clay!

This would be a picture of our best friend of twenty-five years, Mark Evans. We have been through a lot of weird experiences together.

☙17☙

Ain't Bea

1999

When my Aunt Bea passed away on August 4, 1999, I was unable to attend her funeral because my husband Mark and I were in Las Vegas on a trip. I felt extremely disappointed because she was my favorite aunt, and I was exceptionally close to her. I couldn't undo what had already been done; however, I could apologize to her and honor her memory in my own way. So when I arrived home, I decided to have some private time to proceed with my own eulogy.

That night I ran a warm bath, locked myself in the bathroom, lit many candles, and talked to my Aunt Bea. I told her how sorry I was for missing her funeral and that I would miss her terribly because I loved her so much. I thanked her for all that she was, not only to me, but to the rest of the family.

She gave so much of herself, even financially, to help not only everyone in the family but strangers as well. A very good person, I looked up to her. I strive to be like her—strong and giving. She was in a way like Opies' Aunt Bea of Mayberry

with the exception of her naivety. Aunt Bea was everybody's
rock! I told her that I hoped she was in a good place and with
her family that had gone on before her: my cousins, June and
Junior (her children), my Uncle Lewis (her husband), of course,
my grandparents, and all of my aunts and uncles. I asked her if
it were in her power to send me a message to let me know she
was well and okay. A few days later, I received an answer to my
request!

Mark, Evans, and I went out to dine at a Mexican
restaurant in the neighborhood called Chevy's. My husband and
I drove our car, a red Mercedes (I'm not bragging; it's pertinent
to the story), and Evans drove his car. We parked in the same
area of the parking lot but were separated by about twelve cars.
After dinner, we talked and walked (yes, at the same time) to our
cars. My husband strolled several paces ahead of Evans and me.
As usual, Mark and I were deep in conversation, so I wasn't
paying too much attention to the direction in which I walked.
We moved across the parking lot and stopped when we reached
the back of the cars, pretty much dead center between Mark's
car and ours.

Coincidentally, we stopped right behind a cashmere-
colored Infinity QX4—just like our other vehicle sitting at home
in the garage. Evans started ambling in the direction of his car
but paused to watch me. I strode to the right side of the QX4 to
climb into the passenger side of the car, when he said, "You are
going to try to get into that car, aren't you?"

I thought his question was odd, but it jolted me back into
reality as I peered at the license plate of the car and realized that
it wasn't ours. I then remembered that we drove our Benz and

that Mark parked it to the left of where I stood. Evans got a big laugh at my expense, and then we said our good-byes. But as I walked toward our car, I happened to look at the license plate of the car parked next to the QX4. To my surprise, it read "Ain't Bea." I yelled at Evans and said, "Come here!!!" He knew of my Aunt Bea's passing and the fact that I had asked her to give me a sign. He walked over to where I was standing and looked down at the license plate.

In disbelief, he said, "Well, you asked for a sign; there it is.

"I gushed, "Oh my gosh! She did send me a sign!" Very pleased, I said, "Thank you, Aunt Bea!" as I walked to our car where Mark waited patiently. You know what they say, the signs are everywhere! We just need to pay attention to them.

I know that you as a reader have probably experienced an occurrence of this sort, or you probably wouldn't have purchased this book. It's a wonderful feeling to know that our loved ones are still around us and know what is happening in our lives. Often the signs are found on license plates, words we read, words spoken by another, songs on the radio, a television program, or simply a sight or smell. The ways in which we receive the signs are endless. Just believe, have an open mind to the possibility of receiving the messages, and always be grateful for what you receive.

My Aunt Bea was 94 years old when she died. This was
one of the last pictures we took of her.

❧18❧

Wind Chimes

———August 16, 2000———

For well over a month, our wind chimes hanging in the doorway between our kitchen and our laundry room moved at will. No wind or motion on our part aided the movement of the chimes. It was strangely peculiar to stand and watch the wood at the end of the string start swinging like a pendulum and then come to an abrupt stop. The flat piece of wood actually swung side to side just like a pendulum, not around in circles as it would if the air moved it.

Mark, Evans, and I would stand in the kitchen talking, when the wood began to swing. This went on and on. One day while I folded clothes in the laundry room, it started swinging. I looked up at the chimes and said, "Okay, who is playing with the chimes? Is it you, Ed, or you, Jenny?" (This is Evans' deceased father and sister.) Now for the life of me, I don't know why I thought it might be one of them, but that is what came out of my mouth.

I knew what I needed to do next—write down the question "Who is playing with my wind chimes?" on a piece of paper and put it on my nightstand. I then waited and prayed for the answer to come to me in a dream. I thought that I might have a fair chance at receiving an answer, given my history with dreams.

That night I wrote the question on a small piece of paper and put it on my nightstand. I said a little prayer that God would send a dream to me that would answer my question. Since so much has happened to me in my dreams, I had every reason to believe that this would work. However, the next morning to my disbelief, I did not receive the dream that I asked for. Disappointed but not discouraged, I would keep trying until I received my answer.

I dressed for work and headed out the door. I entered the car and started the engine. As I did, the radio blared noisily at me. This was a bit disarming to me because I never turn the car off with the radio playing loudly. I always turn the radio down or completely off before I exit the car. Nevertheless, I reached over to turn the radio volume down when I heard the Bette Midler song, "Wind Beneath My Wings," playing. Taken by complete surprise, I was so excited that I *did* get an answer that I could not wait to tell someone. You see, at Jenny's funeral, the family requested that song be played because they felt that it epitomized Jenny's life. However, when the song was played, it brought them to their knees with grief. Distraught at seeing my friends in such pain, I had wished that they had not played the song.

I picked up my cell phone as I backed out of the garage and dialed, "Evans, it's me. Are you busy?" Evans was still in the office and hadn't gone out into the field yet, so I told him, "It's your sister Jenny; she's the one who's been playing with the wind chimes!

" He asked me how I knew it was her, and I told him the whole story. Evans said, "It is Jenny! It's Jenny!

"I asked him, "Did Jenny like wind chimes or something?" He said he didn't know. So then, I asked him when his mother Helen was coming in to work this week, and he told me that his mother would be in on Thursday. Helen worked in our laundry part time to help us out and to add a little extra money to her pocketbook. I asked him not to mention a word to her about this. I knew that I could trust Evans with my life, so I wasn't worried about him talking to his mother until I had a chance to speak with her myself.

Our building has three stories with our offices on the top floor, the showroom on the main floor, and the laundry in the basement. Helen never failed to climb three flights of stairs at the end of her workday to come in to my office to chitchat for a while and then go to her son's office to tell him good-bye. The most caring and giving person that I know, she always likes to discuss her dreams with me and asks me to help her analyze them. Anyway, Thursday she walked into my office and sat down in a chair in front of my desk. "Hi, Lin," she said as always.

We exchanged a few words and then I queried, "Helen, can I ask you a question?"

She said nonchalantly, "Yeah, what?"

I said tentatively, "Do you know if Jenny liked wind chimes?"

Not surprisingly, she said, "Oh gosh, yes, she had them hanging all over her house!"

I laughed and told her the whole story. Delighted, she said that she needed to go out and buy her own wind chimes, so that Jenny could talk to her.

This is one of the most fulfilling ways in which a spirit can use you to convey a message to another person. I can't tell you the amount of love that is felt in one of these exchanges. So if something unusual happens, no matter how silly it may seem to you, pass the story along; you may be surprised at how important it is to someone else. The unconditional love is felt by all of the constituents.

Through our close friend Mark, we have become friends with his mother, Helen Evans. This is Helen and her daughter Jenny Lynn Evans Hearty.

❧**19**❧

A Candle for Joyce

———October 1, 2001———

On the last day of September, I informed Mark that I intended to light a candle for his mother, Joyce, on the following day, which would be the tenth anniversary of her death. I felt a strong desire to honor Joyce and to let her know that we had not forgotten her.

When I got up the next morning, one of the first things I did was to light the candle. I placed the candle on our nightstand in the relationship corner of our bedroom. I believe in the power of Feng Shui and how it affects every aspect of our life. So, I use specific areas in every room of our house to improve the flow of energy for a healthier and more prosperous life. To learn more about this, you need to pick up a book or two on Feng Shui.

As I lit the candle, I said a little prayer for Joyce and talked to her. I told her that I was lighting a candle in honor of her birthday—a slip of the tongue; what I meant to say, of course, was that I was lighting a candle in honor of her life, since she died on this day. Her birthday was on July 1. I wished her well and told her that I hoped she was happy where she was and progressing forward in the spirit world.

When I explained what I said to my husband later on in the day, he commented that her death was a birthday of sorts. She shed her body in this life to be born again in a new life. I felt much better when he pointed this out to me.

The candle burned most of the day and into the evening. Mark sat down in his recliner in the bedroom to watch a little television before bedtime, and he glanced over at the candle. I explained to him that it was the candle that I lit for his mother and that I allowed the candle to burn all day and well into the evening.

We watched the John Edward's show *Crossing Over* until it ended, and then we switched off the television. We kissed each other and said I love you as we usually did, but this time something else was added. As I said I love you to Mark, someone whispered, "Thank you," loudly into my ear. I even felt their breath blow against my cheek and hair. Automatically, I said, "Did you hear that?"

He said, "What?"

Realizing the message was whispered in my ear and probably just meant for me, I just said, "Never mind," and laid down to go to sleep. Now, it does seem at times that it takes a brick to hit me in the head, but I don't always put two and two together when these things happen to me. I repeated the same story to several people after that, but it wasn't until I recounted it to our friend, Jean Walters, that it hit me—yes, like a ton of bricks! We met with Jean a couple of days after it happened. I was telling her about it when I stopped in mid-sentence and exclaimed, "Oh my goodness! It was Joyce; she was thanking me for lighting a candle for her!" Jean laughed at my astonishment and, I'm guessing, at the stupid look on my face. She agreed with me that no matter how often it happens, it is always a surprise and a totally hair-raising experience that leaves you in awe.

Besides being a very good friend, Jean Walters is a personal-growth consultant, certified-reality therapist, lecturer, and writer.

This is a picture of Joyce, my mother-in-law taken in 1980.

ೞ20☙

Séance

──────January 26, 2007──────

We arrived at the Cassadaga Hotel at two p.m. on Friday. Mark, Evans, and I quickly looked around before entering the hotel to check in at the front desk. Our friend Ron Schulte booked Mark and me the infamous room 10 (known to be the one of most haunted rooms in the hotel). Ron booked Evans into room 22 also a very active room. We did not know much about the hotel, only what Ron previously told us (which wasn't much). We quickly checked in and headed to our rooms to unpack and get settled. While unpacking, I decided to take a few pictures of the room, something I usually do when we travel.

Next, the three of us decided to walk around Cassadaga and check out the area. Across the street from the hotel was the Cassadaga Camp Bookstore. We spent two hours in the bookstore—and about 170 dollars. It was a fascinating place, one that I would have loved to spend more time and money in.

After taking our purchases to our rooms, we opted to ride around the town. We found ourselves driving to Daytona Speedway, walking around there for several hours, taking pictures, buying souvenirs, and having dinner at the restaurant in the Hilton Hotel. Darkness covered the town by the time we started back to Cassadaga. When we arrived at the hotel, there were no cars in the parking lot—not one single person in the hotel! We were all alone in a Haunted Hotel! They told us when we checked in that the hotel staff goes home at night, but we didn't realize that *all* of the staff would leave! That's why they gave us a key to the front door, duh? What had we gotten ourselves into? Did I mention that this was a Haunted Hotel?

The three of us sat in the lobby of the hotel and watched, of all things, *Ghost Whisperers* on the only television in the whole place. Oh, and they didn't place telephones in any of the rooms either; I guess they didn't want any unnecessary phone calls in the middle of the night from any of the terrified guests. I decided that it might be a good idea to grab the camera and take some pictures in the dark. In case there were a few spirits lurking around, I wanted proof!

At approximately ten o'clock, other hotel guests started arriving, one by one. That was somewhat comforting, except that they didn't wish to socialize at all. The guests—cyclists—appeared wiped out. The three of us retired shortly after they came into the lobby. On the main floor not too far from the lobby, a ghostly quiet pervaded our rooms all night.

As we lay in bed conversing about the day's events, we waited for something "paranormal" to happen, but it never did. However, after sleeping an hour or so (Mark said it was about one o'clock in the morning), I awoke suddenly out of a sound sleep. A white oval picture (or sketch) of a lion with its mane hovered over the middle of the room. Over the top of the picture was an arch of purple like a wide brushstroke. The color purple seemed to hold the picture. Mesmerized by the site, I squinted to get a better look, when it disappeared. Unable to believe what I had seen, I didn't know what to make of it. Mark asked me what was wrong because I sat in bed, staring at what appeared to be nothing. I explained to him what I had seen, and then we both went back to sleep. Since the rest of the night was uneventful, we ended up having a rather peaceful night.

In the morning, we headed into the dinning room to eat a light breakfast. We were scheduled to meet with Ron and Raine, our trusty friends, at around half past eleven before our séance appointment at noon. Following that, we would all go to meet with our individual psychics at quarter past two.

Ron and Raine arrived on time, and we stood in front of the hotel and talked until it was time for us to walk to the Colby Temple for our séance. The Temple was just down the street, so it didn't take much time to get there. The five of us—Ron, Raine, Evans, Mark, and I—waited outside of the Temple for our medium, Victor Vogemitz, to arrive. A short time passed, and then Victor and his wife (and his assistant), Ester, arrived and introduced themselves. Victor informed us that we were about to experience table tipping. This left Ron incredulous because Ron's first table tipping experience happened when he was only ten years old. He had no idea that the séance would be the same as table tipping. Victor filled us in on the procedure and explained that the room can get quite cold, when the spirits start coming through.

After hearing this, Mark and Ron went to the cars to get some jackets. While they were gone, Victor continued to explain how he would perform the séance. He looked at me and said, "I will say something like I see two female energies standing behind you. They are the same height as you." Then, Victor looked at me and asked, "Who passed from a stomach ailment?" I thought he was still describing his séance procedures, so I just looked at him.

Then, he repeated himself, "Who passed from a stomach ailment?"

Not thinking clearly at the time, I said, "I don't know." ?Just then, Ron and Mark came back with the jackets. We put them on. Before we went into the Temple, Ron wanted to say a prayer over us for protection before we started, which he did. Victor stated, "I will also say prayers before we start."

We followed Victor and Ester into the Colby Temple, winding around the pews and into a room in the front directly behind the pulpit, referred to as the Heart of the Temple. It was a small room with no windows and only one door. Several chairs were arranged around a 48-inch, round, wooden table; two tall cones stood along the back wall with one in the middle of the wooden table next to a small horn. These objects (trumpets) were all painted with glow-in--dark paint, so that they could easily be seen when all of the lights were turned off. Victor explained to us that in the past, these trumpets were often used by the spirits for communicating purposes and that they were common tools that mediums use for communication. They have been known to float in the air, and voices have spoken out of them directly. He informed us that the spirits use the wooden table as a communicative tool. Victor told us to take our places around the table with husbands and wives sitting next to one another. We sat around the table in the following order: Raine, Ron, Victor, Mark, Linda, and Evans. Outside of the group, Ester sat in a chair along the wall behind Raine, so she could easily assist Victor in turning the lights on or off. Victor instructed Ester to lock the door and turn the lights down slowly ...

Our session started with Victor saying a prayer for protection. We were then asked to say the Lord's Prayer aloud. Victor explained that we would sing songs periodically to help elevate our energy levels, which would also aid the spirits coming through. Once our prayers were finished, we stopped holding hands and placed our hands lightly on top of the table. Victor advised us to let the table move freely under our hands and let our hands glide over the top. Victor instructed us to begin singing "In the Garden," an old Baptist hymn. Immediately, the table started spinning right and left and then immediately went toward Raine. (The first time that I typed this sentence, Raine's name came up on the screen as Loraine; I don't know how, but it did. I only knew her as Raine because that is how Ron introduced us.) The trumpet in the middle of the table began rocking and tipping.

Both Victor and Ester said, "Oh, don't let it fall on the floor, or the connection will be broken." Ester grabbed the trumpet, just as it was ready to fall. The table pushed right up into Raine's midsection. Raine became hysterical; she started laughing and crying at the same time. The rest of us could not believe our eyes. *Could this 100 lb wooden table be moving around on its own?* It could, and it was! Raine started saying,

"It's my dad. Oh, it's my dad! I love you too, Dad, and I miss you so much. I know, I know."

Once I realized what was happening, I began to sob uncontrollably. I was so happy for Raine that I was overrun with emotion. Raine is usually very quiet and reserved. To see her like this, so vulnerable with her emotions all exposed, made my heart go out to her. I could not believe it. *Is this for real?* All of a sudden, the table flipped down on its side with the edge of the top resting on the floor. It moved up to Raine and started hugging her. Yes, that is what I said; it began hugging her! I have never in my life seen anything like this! The table literally became animated. The table's four feet stemming from each pedestal leg (there were two pedestals) would rub up and down her as though affectionately embracing her. It was entirely astonishing! The table started rocking back and forth, as though it were rocking a small child to console it. There were many sounds of disbelief from the rest of us seated around the table. This was truly an experience that none of us had ever had or even imagined having. In my wildest dreams, I could have never come up with this story.

Before Raine's dad passed away, he had so many tubes in his throat that he was unable to speak. He could not tell Raine good-bye or that he loved her. This bothered Raine for a very long time. Now, here he was using this heavy wooden table to get his message across to Raine. Raine informed us later that the song "In the Garden" was one of her dad's favorite songs. Once Raine's dad's energy was gone, the men were able to pick the table up and put it back into its original position. (While the energy controlled the table, there was no budging it.)

Immediately, the table started spinning back and forth, just as it did before. This time, the table went straight to Ron. It pressed so hard up against Ron that it pushed him against the wall. Ron asked if this energy was that of Jake (his grandfather). The table nodded that yes it was. Ron had not seen his grandfather in 30 years, and he was not able to go to his funeral. Ron asked his grandfather a question about a picture that had been taken the last time Ron and his family were with him. The picture was of Ron holding his small son Jake with Ron's dad and his grandfather Jake sitting in front of them. Ron had tried on numerous occasions to see if the baby was laughing or crying in the picture. He even used a magnifying glass to see the baby's face. Still, he could not tell. He asked his grandfather if baby Jake was smiling. The table reared back and nodded yes. The table was on its side at this time (that is to say that the table's top edge was on the floor). After conversing with his grandfather for a short time, Ron did a wonderful thing; he asked his grandfather if he could help the other energies (our relatives) to come through. The table then moved in and hugged Ron, trying to get even closer to him, and then the energy left. Once the energy was gone, the guys picked up the table and put it back on its feet and into the middle of the group.

Victor then instructed us to sing another song. It was a spiritual song, but none of us knew it, so he and Ester sang the song. He then had us sing, "She'll Be Coming Around the Mountain." (Just as a little insight, Mark's mother lived in Phoenix, Arizona, which is very close to Camel Back Mountain.) We started singing the song, and the table spun around wildly and then tipped back and forth. It seemed that all of the songs that we sung were appropriate for that particular spirit. I am positive that Victor as a medium was instructed by his guides to pick the songs that we sang.

The table started moving in Mark's direction. For the first time, I realized that the energies (spirits) retain the personalities that they had while here in the physical world. I heard the medium John Edward talk about this on his show, *Crossing Over*. I believed John Edward when he made the claim. But now, it was proved to me in this séance. The table went up to Mark, touched him, and then pulled back. It did this a couple of times, and Victor asked Ester if she had ever seen anything like this before. She replied, "No."

They did not know Joyce like we did. This epitomized her personality. This was definitely Joyce's spirit! When Joyce was alive, she would get so excited that she could not control her enthusiasm, and she would act kiddy like that. Anyone that knew Joyce could certainly recognize this as her spirit. When she was energized about something, she would wave her arms above her head and flail them around. Mark said, "Hi, Mom!" and then wiped his eyes. He, like his mother, could not control his emotions and found it hard to speak. He managed to tell her he loved her, and he thanked her for coming to me in my dreams. Then he said, "I just can't think," a very common occurrence when you are overcome with emotions. I took over and started talking to Joyce. At this time, the table laid down on its side (tabletop on the floor).

The table turned, looked at me, and looked back at Mark. It then moved up to me and tried to hug Mark and me at the same time. In doing so, it pinned my leg between my chair and the table leg. The table started rubbing up and down my shin. I endured the pain for a while, but then finally, I said, "Ouch!" When I said that, the table quickly moved away as though I startled it. I said, "Its okay!" And I swiftly tucked my feet and legs under my chair. The table came back to me and got right up into my face. I felt like it was trying to climb up onto me; when in fact, it was just trying to get as close as possible. Joyce's spirit used the table because she had no physical body to use. I began to ask questions. "Did Joyce make the gold Christmas ornament fly off of the tree?" I queried. The table nodded yes, very fast, as if to say, "Yes, yes, it was me; I did that!" I knew it was her, but this was a very worthwhile confirmation. I thanked her and told her that I loved her for doing that. It was a gift of pure love when I needed it the most. I then asked her for confirmation on the get-up issue, and again the table nodded yes. I thanked her once again, this time for all of the signs that she gave us acknowledging that she was still present. I told her how grateful I was for all that she taught me and thanked her for the remarkable love that she gave. At this point, I cried very hard, but I kept on talking to her. I thanked her for using me to tell Mark that she loved him; it was very powerful and extremely effective. This whole time, the table leg rubbed up and down my leg. I would describe this feeling as somewhat like embracing someone tightly, while patting them on the back at the same time. I asked Joyce if she came to me, while I was sleeping, and radiated that she loved me by using gold fairy dust that covered me from my head to my waist.

The table again nodded yes very fast, once more as if to say, "Yes, yes, that was me!" She seemed very pleased with the idea that I got it and that I knew it was her. I explained to her that I was extremely sad that she had to make a last visit to me, but I knew it was time for her to move on. I kept telling Joyce that I loved her and was very appreciative for all of the times she sent me messages. I felt bad for Mark because he was unable to speak. He just did not know what to say. So, I asked Joyce to give Mark a big hug because I really felt that he needed it. Almost before, I got all of the words out of my mouth, the table moved quickly back to Mark and gave him a hug. It was very heartwarming and touched everyone present. Mark thanked his mother for coming through and changing our lives so drastically. Joyce did not want to leave. To repeat what I said earlier, when the spirit has control of the table, you absolutely cannot budge it. Finally, the table could be moved; so once again, the guys picked it up and put it back into place.

Victor said, "Okay, it's time for another song. Let's sing 'You Are My Sunshine.'" Through the whole song, I prayed that my grandma would come through. I did not realize at the time that the songs that we sang were the appropriate songs for our spirits. That song was for me from my grandma. Victor said, "Who passed from a stroke? Not a heart attack, a stroke; I am getting a pain on the right side of my head and that indicates a stroke."

I ecstatically exclaimed, "That's my grandma!! Oh my gosh, she's coming through!" I was so overwhelmed with excitement that I started crying profusely, and I did NOT care! The table immediately got right up in my face; this was a big hug from my grandma. Sobbing, I asked her if she remembered our last day together, when she walked without her cane and helped me make cinnamon rolls from scratch.

Victor inserted, "So, that's what I smell!"

The table nodded yes; my grandma did remember that day. I asked her if she really was the one who touched me on my shoulder, while I was doing dishes at the kitchen sink. The table once again affirmed that it was her. Through my tears, I thanked her for coming to me, and I told her how much I loved and missed her. I told Grandma how sorry I was for what happened between my mom and me. I said, "I have tried very hard to turn the other cheek and continue to be a good daughter, but nothing I do seems to help. I love Mom very much, but I just do not know what else to do."

Victor added, "Your grandmother said she will help you by being a bridge between you and your mother toward better communication."

Now, how do I know that this statement came from my grandmother and not from Victor? Because Victor could not possibly know about my mother, he could not have known that my mother's biggest problem is with communication. He could not know how my mother twists the truth around to suit herself. This statement could have only come from my mother's mother. I asked Grandma to visit Mom in a dream. At this time, Victor pointed out just how much popping and cracking the table was doing. He explained to us that this is how the spirit uses the table to talk to us. With all the moaning and groaning coming from the table, it was easy to visualize my grandma consoling me and trying to sooth my pain.

I then asked Grandma if my Uncle Buel, Granddad, and the others were there with her. The table (still on its side) turned left and right as though it was looking for the person or people that I asked about. At this particular moment, the séance really became wild because all of my family started coming through.

For the second time, Victor replied, "Who passed from a stomach ailment?" You may recall that while we were still outside waiting to start the séance, Victor asked me this question, although I did not have an answer. However, once we started conversing with our deceased relatives, my mind was in the correct frame, so I knew immediately who it was.

I said, "My Uncle James passed from stomach trouble. Oh, it's my Uncle James! He was a funny man!" My mind spun, and I tried to think of what to say. Now, I realized what my husband was going through when his mother came to him; your mind goes blank. The table came up and hugged me again. I asked Uncle James if he remembered giving a ride to my two young sons around on his lawn mower in his front yard, when they were two and three years old. Of course he did, they do not lose their memories, but it was something to say when I had nothing else. The table nodded yes. Unfortunately, I did not get the chance to spend much time with my Uncle James, as I didn't know what else to say. So, I asked him if Uncle Buel was there with him.

This prompted Ester to say, "Oh, he is going to think you are rude; he came through to talk to you."

This made me feel terrible; there is no way I wanted to insult my family, but this was my first séance. I had never done this before. I prayed that he forgave me because I didn't even think that he might have something to tell me. I know now why he was so anxious to come through. When his wife, my Aunt Carrie, lost their son Jimmy on April 1, 1995, she was devastated. I talked to her at his funeral and tried to explain to her that I know that life is eternal and that she can still talk to Jimmy. I even sent her the book *We Don't Die*. Or I thought that he might have wanted to let me know something about his stomach problems because his daughter Pat is now having problems with her stomach, and the doctors cannot figure it out.

Either way, I will keep the door open for my Uncle James, so that his message will eventually get through to me. I asked Uncle James again if Uncle Buel or Granddad was there with him. There was a slight delay.

Then Victor started sniffing the air and finally said, "Do I smell smoke?

Why am I smelling smoke?"

I knew it was my granddad. I told Victor that it was my grandfather coming through; I am reminded of him every time I smell wood burning. When my granddad was alive, he would always be the first to rise in the morning. When the house was cold, he would always put wood into the wood-burning stove to take the chill out of the air before everyone else got up. So, he always smelled like firewood or wood burning. It is actually quite a wonderful aroma, one that always takes me back to my childhood and Grandma's house. My granddad was a shy man and never spoke much, but he always had a smile for me. He would tease me every now and then; this was his way of playing with his grandchildren. On occasion, I would sit next to him at the dinner table, and he would grab at my food as if he was going to take it just to get a rise out of me. This was the most contact that I had with him. So when I spoke to my granddad's energy, I apologized for not taking the time to get to know him better.

Victor said that I had many spirits lined up behind me, waiting to talk to me.

Victor continued, "Who was real shaky?"

I knew instantly that it was my Uncle Buel. I said, "That is my Uncle Buel; he had sugar diabetes and would get shaky when his blood sugar was low." I was elated that Uncle Buel finally came through—not that I did not want to talk to the others, I did, but Uncle Buel was like a dad to me; he made me feel loved and wanted. I was around him much more than any of my other uncles. The table came up and hugged me. I began thanking Uncle Buel for loving me, caring for me so well, including me in his family, and taking me with them every time they would go to the country (Advance, MO) to see my cousin's grandma, Granny. If he brought a shinny, new, half dollar home to his daughter Charollet than I would get one too. He never made me feel left out or in the way. I asked Uncle Buel if he could see his daughter Charollet (his one and only child), and the table nodded yes. I asked him if he could also see his grandchildren and great-grandchildren. The table shook a lot, showing his excitement and his sense of humor, and then nodded yes. I told him how very happy I was for her, especially that she finally had that big family she always wanted. Growing up as an only child was very lonely for her. A good person, she deserves to be happy; I know in my heart that nothing makes her happier than her family.

I then realized that I had taken so much time with my relatives. I was concerned over the time that we had left. I told

Uncle Buel that I loved him and thanked him for coming through. I also thanked all of my relatives at that point and told them that I loved them and appreciated all they contributed to my life. The table quickly slid backwards (still on its side), so far from me that I had to stretch to keep a hand on the foot of the pedestal. It pushed the people on the opposite side all the way back to the wall. The table then tilted back, until I could see the whole underside of the tabletop, and it began to quiver non-stop. No one knew what was taking place, so Victor filled us in.

He said, "The table backed up and tilted back, so that all of her family could see her, and they are now sending her love and healing energy. Oh, they are very proud of you, how you have managed your life, and what you have accomplished."

I could not believe what I heard, and I certainly did not know how badly I needed to hear those words. For a very long time, I have received nothing but grief from my mother, brother, and my two sons. It seems that in their eyes, I can do nothing right. I haven't seen or spoken to my brother in over eight years (his choice, not mine). My mother is constantly belittling me, and my oldest son blames me for all of his bad choices (a duplicate of my mother). My youngest son moved out of the country with no plans of returning. The love, admiration, and support that I do have comes from my husband, a few good friends, and from my family on the other side. It's nice to know that I do have family members who care and watch over me with unconditional love.

While all of this was going on, Victor said to Ron, "Try to move this table." Ron strained against the table, but it would not budge. Victor continued, "You won't be able to move it until they [the spirits] are all finished."

Sometime during this conversation, my stomach started aching. At first, I thought it was hunger pains, but I quickly realized that the pain was not from lack of food. Two areas of sharp pain radiated throughout my midsection. I now believe that it was my Uncle James, trying to come through again! I felt that it was quite possible that he still had a message for me. My suspicion proved to be right. Although I did not get the chance to talk to him again in this séance, he reappeared in our second séance. When my family released the table, the guys picked it up and sat it back on its feet in the middle of the circle.

From the other side of the table, Victor instructed us to sing "I've Been Working On the Railroad." Once again, the table spun back and forth, left to right. While the table moved, Victor asked, "Who had ringing in their ears?"

Nonchalantly, Evans said, "My dad had ringing in his ears." I looked at Evans in disbelief because although I have known him for almost thirty years, I never knew that—or any of the information that was to follow. The table moved over to Evans, but instead of turning on its side with the bottom of the table facing him (as the table did with the rest of us), it turned the opposite way. This was something new; the top of the table faced Evans with the feet pointed away from him. The table then backed away from Evans; the top lifted off the floor, back down again, off the floor, and back down again. It did this several times just as effortlessly as you would move your head up and down to view someone from head to toe. Victor stated that this is exactly what Mark's dad was doing. He looked

Evans up and down because he could not believe how much he had changed.

Victor said, "Has he been gone for a long time?" Evans answered that he'd been gone since 1984. Victor said sometimes when the table tilts that way you can see the spirit's face in the top of the table. The table then moved closer to Mark Evans and started vibrating incredibly fast. As it did, it made a tapping sound on the floor.

Victor asked Mark, "What is the mechanic connection?"

Mark's answer surprised us all, "My dad started out as a mechanic on the railroad, and then worked as a fork-lift mechanic."

(*Didn't we just finish singing, "I've Been Working On the Railroad?" Geez!!*) The whole time the table made the tapping noise on the floor. But as soon as Mark revealed his dad's early vocation, the sound turned from a tapping to a rumble. In other words, the car finally started, and we all finally got it! This is exactly why we should be using more than 10% of our brains! Just think of how many times we have missed messages from the other side because we ignored the signs. Evans asked his dad if he came to him in a dream where he was driving his corvette. The table nodded very quickly, "Yes, yes." Evans dreamed this shortly after his dad passed. In his dream, while he drove, his dad called him on his cell phone. Aware even while dreaming that his dad died, he quickly asked his dad, "Where are you? Stay there; I'll be right there." In the dream, his dad told him, "No, I've got to go," and then the phone went dead.

Evans asked his dad to watch over his mother, Helen, and younger sister, Kim, and brother, Kirk. He requested that his dad visit Kirk in a dream, knowing that it might heal Kirk's broken heart and guilty feelings. Before Evans' dad died, Kirk and he argued without resolving their disagreement. Kirk has never been able to move past it.

Victor then said, "He is telling me baseball. What does that mean?"

Evans answered, "When Dad was alive, he used to take me to all of the St. Louis Cardinal's baseball games. Hey, Dad, tell Grandpa Evans that I found what he hid in his *Life* Magazines!" Evans was referring to a First Nighters' Certificate to the first game played at the New Busch Stadium built in the early 1960s. Evans added, "I have a First Nighters Certificate too from the New Busch Stadium built in 2006."

Evans inquired about his sister Jenny, who passed suddenly at the age of 28. Jenny played on a soccer team and was injured in one of the games. She tore a ligament in her knee and needed to have arthroscopic surgery. She lived in a rural town in Illinois, and her doctor of choice opted to put a cast on her leg from the hip to the ankle. It is believed that she developed a blood clot due to the surgery, which traveled to her heart and caused her sudden death. Evans asked his dad if Jenny was there with him, and the table nodded yes. Evans told his dad that he loved him and would now like to speak with Jenny. The table backed up and began to vibrate very fast. As we learned earlier, his dad was sending him healing energy. At some point in time, the table turned and tilted away from Evans because his dad used the table to hug him, just as the other spirits. Once the vibrating ended, Evans' dad's energy was gone. The guys once again righted the table and put it back where it belonged.

However, the table did not stay there long, and we did not have time for another song because the table began spinning immediately. The table became wild and did something quite different from before. It toyed with going up to Evans, but then it went to Victor. The table then started hopping all around in the middle of the group. Victor said to Evans, "Did someone in your family walk with an unusual gait?"

Confused, Evans didn't answer.

Then Victor said, "Did they walk different than you with a limp?"

Evans said, "I don't know?"

All of a sudden, it dawned on me, I said, "Evans, Jenny had a cast on her leg when she died, so she would walk with a limp!"

Victor then asked about a breathing problem.

Evans told Victor that she had a blood clot travel to her heart, which made it hard for her to breathe. "That's Jenny!" Evans said. The table began hopping all around and spinning wildly, as if Jenny was saying, "Yeah, yeah, it's me!" We laughed and dodged the table at the same time.

Afraid that someone was going to get hurt by the dancing, limping table, Victor said, "Okay, okay, you don't have a cast on your leg anymore, so you don't have to limp. You are fine!"

The table stopped celebrating and moved over to Evans. Then it reared back and shimmied in for a big hug. Evans told his sister that he loved her and missed her a lot. The table began rocking and hugging him as if Jenny said, "Awe, I miss you too!" Evans asked Jenny if she was the one playing with my chimes (Chapter 18). The table nodded wildly as if to say, "Yeah, wasn't that cool!" and then settled back down. Evans asked her if she had something to do with my radio blasting the Bette Midler song, "Wind Beneath My Wings." Once again, the table nodded yes. Evans replied, "That was very clever, Jenny."

Victor said that there was some kind of sisterhood between Jenny and me, and that is why she chose me. I didn't know Jenny—I only met her once at her wedding with Evans. I never saw her again after that until her funeral.

Victor said, "It is because you can laugh and poke fun at Evans, just like sisters do."

That reminded me of the way Evans walks when he gets in a hurry. So I told Victor, "When Evans gets in a hurry, he walks funny. He walks with his head pointed way out in front of his body; he looks like a pull toy." Victor said, "Okay, I get it now, which is why she is showing me a duck on a string. She is telling me that she always has to lay down in front of you, so that you won't trip or step in to the smelly stuff. She says that you always get into the smelly stuff." *Oh, my goodness, that is so Evans! I have known him a very long time, and his sister is so right on!*

Victor then asked Evans if he has been decorating. I said, "Yeah, he just redecorated his whole house.

Victor then added, "She is saying that she did not like something that you did; she would of done it differently."

Evans then asked Jenny if she could see the Florida house, and the table nodded yes quickly. He then asked her to watch over their mother and their sister, Kim. He asked her to go to their mom in a dream and to ring her chimes!

Victor said, "She is saying that she did not want to scare her mother."

Evans said, "You won't scare her; that's why she bought the chimes."

The table quieted down, and the guys were able to set the table upright. All of the orbs that had been in the room from the beginning started to fade. We thought that we were finished, when the table began to spin once again. We were all confused because everyone had heard from their loved ones' spirits. This time, the table went straight to Victor. Victor said, "You know you are not supposed to come to the medium." Victor asked, "Who are you? Is it..." He proceeded to name about three different people. It was his grandfather Hernan C. Vogenitz, who wanted Victor to check on someone by the name of Paul. Victor commented, "We went by his house, but he was gone to lunch. We will go by and check on him on the way home." Victor continued, "While we still have all of the spirits here, let's see if we can raise the table over our heads." He instructed us to stand that proved to be a little bit difficult for some of us because we were all drained of our energy. It took more of our energy than we had expected to bring the spirits through. As we stood and put our hands lightly on top of the table, Victor requested the spirits to help us lift the table up over our heads.

The table began to move in a spinning motion and then came up off the floor. We tried three times to lift it higher but never got it more than three feet off the floor. Later, we found out that one of us put pressure on the table. I can't imagine a 100 lb table lifting three feet off the floor by itself, but it did.

We sat back down in our seats and sang a closing song, "Happy Trails to You," a Roy Rodgers and Dale Evans signature song. Victor then closed with a prayer. This was to close the gates to the spirit world. Ester turned the lights up slowly. As Victor sat directly across from Evans, he opened his eyes to see a seven-foot, blue, master guide, standing behind Evans. Ester commented that it had been there the whole time. As we all stood up, the guide walked right through Evans and stood in front of him to protect him. Victor stated that the master guide was there to guide Evans to a higher spiritual level. *Okay, great! What about our guides, where are they, and what color are they?*

Victor looked over at Ron and said, "You have been living too much in the future and not enough in the present. Try having more fun and living in the present." Victor then turned to Raine and me and said, "You girls get it!" We left right away to get to our appointments at quarter past two. It was already 2:07 p.m.

On our first night at the Cassadaga Hotel, at approximately 1:30 a.m., I awoke to to see this image floating in mid-air, in the center of the room. I know that the color purple has always been equated with royalty, and the lion to me could mean courage, but I am not positive about the meaning.

**Our friend Mark Evans standing in front of the Cassadaga
Hotel.**

The Colby Temple, built in 1923 was named after the founder of the Cassadaga Spiritual Camp, George P. Colby. All of our séances take place here.

In the year of 1957 my grandmother and granddad celebrated their sixtieth wedding anniversary

My Uncle James entertaining my two young sons, by riding them around on his lawn mower in 1972.

Henry A. Hood, my granddad was a hard working man, and it was said, that he would give you the shirt off of his back, if you needed it.

My Uncle Buel was a very important part of my life, as he
displayed plenty of love, protection, and security for a child
who had very little self-esteem. This is a very old picture
of my Uncle Buel, my Aunt Almeada and my cousin
Charollet, but it was a time that was most important to me.

Jenny and her father, Ed Evans, on her wedding day, May 5, 1984. Ed passed away in November of the following year, 11/19/85. Jenny Lynn Evans Hearty, joined her father on April 18, 1990, at the age of twenty-eight.

❧ 21 ❧

Return to Cassadaga

——March of 2007——

O ur first visit to Cassadaga turned out to be such a life-changing experience that we opted to return for a second time. So on March 16 and 17 of 2007, Mark, Ron, Raine, and I drove up to the town of Cassadaga. The drive there was a blast. We laughed the whole way. Everyone was in rare form, so it was quite the adventure. Since our last visit was so phenomenal, we knew what to expect this time. Our only worry was how we were going to top our last visit there. But as we soon found out, we didn't have to worry because the spirits had it all under control. Mark drove, and unlike the first time, he got lost. It wasn't his fault, however. Many of the roads were under construction, and we simply made a wrong right turn instead of a left turn. Because we drove too far in the wrong direction, we were confused and didn't know where we were. So, we pulled into a gas station to ask for directions. I might add that Raine and I didn't have a problem with asking, so of course we went in and got directions. Guys are so childish!

We walked into the station. Both clerks behind the counter busily helped other customers; we stood and waited our turn. However, the clerks were not in any hurry. So after about five minutes, I asked, "Could someone tell us how to get to Cassadaga from here?" One of the customers that just concluded her business turned around and said she could. When she looked up at us, I was convinced that I knew her from somewhere. I said, "You look so familiar to me. Have you ever been to Naples?"

She said, "Yeah, you look familiar to me too; your eyes look familiar, but no, I've never been to Naples." We couldn't figure out how we knew each other, so we dropped it. She pointed us in the right direction, and we left.

While driving, I filled the guys in on our discussion with the lady in the station and commented that I wished I could have figured out where I had seen her before. Because I had a past-life regression scheduled as soon as we got to Cassadaga, Raine remarked, "Don't worry; you'll figure it out soon." Timing is everything!

We arrived at the hotel with little time to spare. Jamie (the medium I had the appointment with) waited for me. We checked into our room (room #10 again), and Jamie led me to her office.

I was a little nervous because I had never been hypnotized before, and I didn't think I could be because I am so hyper. Jamie managed to get me totally relaxed, and even though I didn't feel like I was under hypnosis (Jamie explained that I would still be aware of what I was saying and to just say the first thing that came to mind), I later believed that I was.

Jamie first asked me to open my eyes and tell her what I saw. When I opened my eyes, I saw small children playing. They ran around the yard with sticks in their hands and rolled big hoops. There was no grass, just dirt. Jamie then asked me where I was. I told her I stood in front of my house. She told me to look around and see if I knew where my house was, but I didn't know. She asked me if I was a boy or girl, and I didn't answer her. She said, "How old are you?" I answered that I was six years old. She told me to look down at my clothes and tell her what I wore. When I looked down, I saw that my shirt was buttoned wrong, and I tried to hide it. I told her that I had on short pants, a shirt, and no shoes. She asked me what color my hair was, and I didn't know because I never saw the color of my hair. I tried to pull my hair down in front of my eyes so that I could see it but couldn't. I guessed the color and said blonde. Jamie asked me what color my skin was. I said, "Skin color." She told me to go into my house, look around at the furnishings, and tell her what I saw. I didn't see much of anything. She asked me where I slept, and I told her, "Over in that corner."

Jamie then told me to go forward in time a few years to a special event that meant a lot to me. She said, "What is going on?"

I told her, "It's my wedding day. I am arm in arm with my girl."

"What is her name?"

I replied, "Susie."

She then asked me where we were, and I answered her, "In a building."

She asked me where I lived, and I told her Arkansas. She then told me to go ahead to the day I died. I went to the day she instructed me to go to. I started to cry because I saw myself lying on the ground surrounded by the fall leaves with my arms and legs turned backwards. I could see the hindquarters of a horse. Jamie asked me if anyone was there with me or if I was alone. I told her I was alone. She asked me if I was old. I told her, "No, I am not old; I am too young to die."

That is the only past-life regression that I have had. I left feeling disappointed because I did not expect that outcome. I guess I had a preconceived idea as to what would happen. (It wasn't until later that I realized how perfectly that past life related to my current life). My preconceived idea was that I would regress back to life on a plantation. I've always felt that I was a servant to the mistress of big plantation; I felt that I was a black woman. I have always loved the antebellum-style homes but felt that I didn't live in the big house but in a smaller house in the back. I also feel a connection to the Victorian era.

I now realize how being a small child in poverty conditions living in Arkansas connects to this lifetime. First, my biological father, Joe, came from Arkansas, and they were very poor. Second, I think my low self-esteem may have carried over from that lifetime. Jamie said that we would concentrate on a significant lifetime that would help me in this lifetime.

Our dear friends, Ron and Raine Schulte, who introduced us to Cassadaga, Florida.

This would be my husband, Mark, unpacking for our overnight stay in the Cassadaga Hotel. I always like to take pictures of the rooms we stay in, just for my own reference. It just so happened that I caught a spirit orb which is floating between the two end bedposts, directly to the left of Mark's head.

22

A Motley Crew

———— March 16, 2007 ————

O n our return trip to Casadaga, we decided to take more pictures, since we captured so many interesting orbs and unexplainable objects on film the first time here. After dinner, we waited for nightfall and decided to walk around the campgrounds in search of anything out of the ordinary. With cameras in hand, we headed down to McKinley Street taking pictures here and there. We cut across Seneca Street and stopped to take pictures of Blackhawk Park, the Colby Temple, and Seneca Park. Along the way, we managed to capture quite a few interesting energies on film, including several orbs and even a tiny little boy sitting on a bench. At first, I thought the little guy was an extraterrestrial because his feet and legs looked slightly elongated, but then I thought that he could be of the fairy or gnome realm because he was so tiny. Please look at the picture at the end of this chapter before you start laughing. I took this picture with an ordinary digital camera with absolutely no enhancements, and put it on a picture CD and into a computer to zoom in for a closer look.

We continued our walk down Marion Street, snapping pictures left and right. When we got to Harry Fogel Park, we stopped abruptly looking at the tiny white lights zooming about in all directions. No, they were not fireflies! They were bright, white lights that flew around at lightning speed; yes, if you blinked, you missed them. Since we were told beforehand that this was a healing park, we all believed that we witnessed thousands of spirits (deceased humans) flying around. We did indeed take many photos here. I later did some research and came up with the idea that yes, while they are spirits, they are from other realms, such as the fairy realm. At this point, both Raine and my camera batteries died. Strange, but it is said that the spirits do in fact drain the energy from electronics, and we believe that is exactly what happened in our case.

One of the guys made a comment about how people that are terrified of things that go bump in the night should see what we saw here tonight. We started wondering about how people react to certain "scary" objects and managed to come up with how fast they would run to get away from the ghosts and goblins! The unknown does not exactly frighten Ron, Mark, Raine, and me, but many people are afraid of what they do not understand.

We entertained ourselves by reenacting scenes from the *Little Rascals*. Everyone remembers how adorably funny Buckwheat was when he was frightened. Usually, the show would use other people to poke fun at how silly situations are if viewed from the right perception. Between the *Little Rascals* and the *Three Stooges*, we got a good idea at how to laugh at ourselves. People in wheelchairs rolling down the streets out of control, and grownups on crutches falling down—all of it seemed hysterical, considering it was just slap-stick humor. The shows were not meant to be taken seriously and neither were we.

After having some lighthearted fun, we ventured to the backside of the park and started on around to Spirit Pond. However, as the street lights were placed further apart from one another, and the street ahead of us loomed in the distance, our pace slowed down considerably. Of course, it was mostly due to Raine and me, and the fact that I cannot run as fast as I used to because the guys tried as hard as they could to keep us moving toward Spirit Pond. The girls finally won, and we did an about face and started retracing our steps back the way we came, down Marion Street, where the bright white lights zinged about. But wait, it was much darker now than when we first passed by. One of the street lights had gone out. I guess the spirits needed more energy than our measly camera batteries could provide.

Oh well, it was getting late, and we needed to get back to our rooms in the Cassadaga Hotel. Now, one would think that if I had enough courage to stay in a "haunted" hotel room twice that I could easily walk down a pitch-black street through a heavily wooded area. Nah!!!! As we rounded the Colby Temple and walked back up McKinley Street, we noticed a group of people coming toward us. We had not seen a single person since we turned around and started walking back. Now a group of five people headed our way. We continued talking about the amazing phenomena that we had witnessed as we started closing in on the group. As we got closer, we could not believe our eyes. *Are we seeing things or what?*

The group of people stopped us to ask us if we had seen any ghosts, and if there were any ghost tours occurring. It seems that they had just driven over from Orlando to take a ghost tour. It was half past ten. We told them that we didn't know of any tours going on at the moment because everyone was either gone or in their hotel room. But we did see some rather interesting things, and we pointed them in the direction from which we had come. They thanked us and proceeded to follow our lead.

The four of us looked at each other as if we had seen several ghosts and said, "No way, I don't believe it. How can this happen?" Why, you may ask. Because the five people in the group consisted of a very, very tall, black man, two elderly, oriental women, a pretty, young, black girl on crutches, and a young, Hispanic woman in a wheelchair. Need I say more?

This is another strange occurrence that I can't explain. I am not trained in any field of psychology; I only know what has happened in my life to be, in fact, true. In *The Secret*, John Assaraf states: "You are the most powerful magnet in the universe! You contain a magnetic power within you that is more powerful than anything in this world, and this unfathomable magnet power is emitted through your thoughts." Well, I most certainly agree with that. The four of us proved that to be true!

We walked around Cassadaga at night hoping to catch
spirits on our digital cameras. We managed to catch more
than spirit lights and orbs. In this picture, we captured a
tiny little being that looks like a small boy. He is sitting on
the far right bench, all the way to the right edge, and he is
waving at the camera. He has light colored hair, parted to
one side, and he is wearing a striped shirt with short
sleeves. His little legs and feet look very odd, kind of
elongated. He is seated in front of the Healing Center.

This is the same picture as the previous one, only enlarged several times to enhance the manifestation of the little boy spirit on the bench

23

Séance Two

2007

We once again met Victor (the medium) in front of the Colby Temple, exactly at noon. Ron, Raine, Mark, and I followed Victor to the séance room in the front of the Temple. Our best friend, Evans, could not make this trip with us because he was taking care of our business back in St. Louis. Ester, Victor's wife, also could not be with us because of a shoulder ailment. So it was just the four of us and the medium. This time, Victor remembered to bring his night camera, which he purchased from the *Most Haunted* Web site (a television program on the Travel Channel). This séance was taped on a DVD.

We sat around the wooden table as we waited for Victor to set up the camera. After the last séance, we were yearning for more, especially Ron and Raine. They were so concerned that everyone in the group had enough time with their loved ones' spirits that they didn't take enough time for themselves. Raine needed to converse with her deceased sister, and Ron had some unanswered questions also. Anyway, as we sat there anxiously waiting to get started, I felt a hand brush over the top of my head, which gave me the shivers. As I reacted with an o-o-o-o, Victor explained that it was Sarah, the little girl that loves to come around and play with women's hair.

We started the séance with the Lord's Prayer. Victor immediately followed with a protective prayer. We then repeated three times, "The light of God never fails; the light of God never fails; the light of God never fails. I am the light." Victor then said the table would start to spin clockwise and then counterclockwise, creating a circuit of energy. As this energy begins to move faster and faster, it moves up through the center of the table, up through the ceiling, and all the way to the spirit world. Victor said that our loved ones, friends, and teachers that have passed are seated around a table very much like the one we are seated around, and they send their energy down to us in a counterclockwise motion. Victor continued, "Where the two energies meet between the matter and spirit, they make the connection." We asked our doorkeepers to open the doors and gates to communication.

Victor informed us, "Our purpose here is for communication for the survival of consciousness. This is done with respect and gratitude. Now, we'll take a moment and see the Blue Ray of Healing rise up through the center of the table along the column that is connected to the spirit. This Blue Ray of Healing is connected to the mind, body, and spirit. Situations may arise, which require that special energy. So, as we do this, we will all receive the healing as will our absent loved ones— those that we know need to heal. So, what we'll do is just speak their names and the type of healing that they may need."

Victor mentioned Ester and some others that he knew. After which, I asked for a healing for my sons Troy and Rodney and my mother. Mark next asked for a healing for his dad and his whole family. Next, Raine petitioned for healings for her family with special consideration for her dying mother.

Victor responded, "Now, we see this Blue Ray of Healing filling this room giving each and everyone of us a healing— healing for our minds, our bodies, and our spirits. The healing light rises up out of this room into the temple and into the camp, healing everyone in the camp, healing old animosities and grievances. And the Blue Ray of Healing rises out into the city, healing all of those tornado victims that we had last month, out into the nation, and from the nation into the world. We ask for all of those, who live upon the earth, who are in need of healing. We also ask for planet earth itself to be healed. Please let the earth be returned to the Eden that it once was." Victor concluded with a healing prayer.

Looking at Mark and me, Victor said, "While you were talking, there was the biggest, red-orb flash between the two of you. And if you look, you can see the light in the corner right up against the edge of the wall; there is nowhere that it could be coming from."

I said that the same light was there last time we conducted a séance.

Victor said, "The light has not been here since the last time you were in this room. That light is for you; that is your connection."

Ron offered, "That same light was in the pictures that we took in the hotel," pleasantly reminding us of all the pictures that we took around the hotel and the spirits that we had caught on film.

Victor received a message from beyond that it was time to start. The reminder came in the form of a distant thump that we all heard. Victor commented, "Okay, we'll start." We started singing "In the Garden." The table began moving, spinning as it did in the first séance. Once again, Raine's dad came through first. Immediately, Raine asked her dad if her sister Sheila was there and if she could talk to her. The trumpets on the middle of the table (one large and one small) fell toward Raine. Victor asked Raine if she recognized who was coming through to her.

She said, "I think it's my dad and sister."

Victor replied, "That makes sense. The larger trumpet is your dad, and the smaller one is your sister. They are looking at you, Raine."

Raine started excitedly talking to her sister because Sheila didn't come through in the first séance. Sheila answered her questions via the table. Raine asked, "Sheila, are you the one that has been coming to Mom on her deathbed?" Sheila answered affirmatively. Raine began crying and pleaded with Sheila and her dad to help her mother cross because she was in so much pain.

Victor interjected, "Your dad and sister are there with your mother."

Raine told them, "I know Mom can see you because she looks up and talks to you as if you were physically there. Am I doing the right thing in trying to get the rest of the family to let go of Mom, so she can pass? They are holding her here by feeding her and telling her not to give up, although she is pretty much in a vegetative state." Raine received the answer she needed from her deceased dad and sister. Raine asked them to appear to her brother, James, and explain to him what needed to be done. Distraught, Raine appealed to them on her mother's behalf because her mother was sad, confused, and in an in-between state. She said, "Please help them to understand that she is ready to go home." Raine then asked Sheila, "Can I talk to you about your death?"

Sheila was brutally murdered, and it is their belief that she was an innocent victim caught in the middle of a drug deal gone wrong. The case was never solved, and the perpetrator never found. Raine continues to search for answers.

Ron posed a question to Victor regarding the status of Sheila's crossing. Raine said, "I want to know where Sheila is, and if she is okay."

Victor asked Raine, "You've lost contact with her?"

Raine said, "Yes, but right after Sheila passed, she came to my bedside."

Victor said, "Okay, what happens is you cross over, and you are disoriented; so you look around to see where you are, it takes time. She went to sleep. The Bible got it right when it stated that you go to sleep. It just left out the part where you wake up. So, the reason you haven't heard from Sheila in a while is because she went to sleep to heal. Sheila was very close to you for a little while before she crossed all the way over."

Raine replied, "Yeah, she did come to my bedside."

Victor said, "After that, she went to sleep to heal, and when she woke up, there were people there with her. They call it The Bardo Plane or the Hospital Plane, and it's just a level of healing; there are people there to help with your passing. Just like in the movie (*Defending Your Life* with Meryl Streep)."

The table moved in to hug Raine. Raine said, "I love you too, Sheila."

Victor said, "What's the event that you have coming up here that's related to her?"

"The anniversary of her death is coming up," Raine said. She tried to remember the date that her sister passed, but she drew a blank. She said, "I can't remember." (By the way, this is very common when you are in a séance.)

Sheila wasn't too fond of that response, so the table backed up and looked at Raine as if to say, "You can't remember when I died?" We all laughed because we knew what it felt like when you try to remember certain things in a session like this; it's just not that easy!

Raine said it was about this time of the year when Sheila's son found her in their home. Raine asked, "Can you tell me what happened?"

Victor intervened and said, "Well, it's over, and she's okay."

Raine wanted to know if Sheila's son, Robert, was involved, but Sheila wouldn't answer. So Raine asked her, "Should we try to forgive Robert and pray for him?"

Victor said, "She is saying that this is like a slap in the face; her body is like a car that's been in an accident, and she'll just get out and go to another car." Victor meant that once the accident is over, it's over. You get out and go to another car, and it's just that simple. Victor saw another light on the floor and pointed it out to us. He said, "You guys bring the nicest spirits with you."

Raine asked, "Sheila, is Granny here with you? Have you seen her?" The table shook yes, and we all laughed. Raine then ask Sheila if she met their grandfather, George Monroe McGinnis, because Raine has never met him. The table didn't do anything.

Victor explained to us, "Remember in the Bible where it says, in My mansion there are many rooms! Well, its like we may be in this house with many rooms, and the spirit you are asking about may be in another room."

Raine said, "So, Granny is near you, right?" The table shook yes again.

Victor asked Raine, "Is there anything underneath the table?"

Raine and I both looked and saw a light under the table. Victor said that the table was acting as a protection for all of the energies; they were sending energy to Raine. The table then hugged Raine in an expression of how Sheila emanated love to Raine. Raine said, "I love you too, Sheila! Have you met any of my spirit guides?" The table shook yes, and when Raine asked Sheila if she was one of them, the table shook as if it was saying "Oh, yes!" Raine thanked Sheila for coming through and told her again that she loved her. Raine ask Sheila if she would like to meet her friend, Linda. Victor said that he was just about to fall into the table, meaning that the vortex was extremely deep. Ron started telling Sheila that she needed to get all of her relatives over on the other side together to help the relatives here to understand that Raine's mom is ready to go home and that they need to let her go.

Victor said, "Okay, I am praying from my side; you need to pray from your side too! You know that I've read that when you pray for a spirit, it increases their energy and that they become healthier; it builds up their energy. It helps them rise to the next level.

I had also read that in one of my metaphysical books. It is good to talk to and recognize them. Victor said, "Have you ever see the movie, *The Blue Bird*, with Shirley Temple?"

Raine said, "Sheila and I used to watch Shirley Temple movies all of the time."

Ron added, "We prayed last night that all of our families' spirits would get together and ask God to help us with our wishes."

Victor said, "Hold on; they are letting one spirit step out of the table, so that another can step in. Tell you what, let's sing 'I've Been Working on the Railroad.'" This is the song that we sang in the first séance that brought Evans' dad through. We sang the song, and Victor commented, "We probably won't make it on American Idol! Who is the person that passed from emphysema or lung problems that caused them to cough all of the time?"

I said, "My Aunt Margaret passed from emphysema." After I made that statement, the table quickly moved over to me and flipped onto its side. In total disbelief, I realized that I didn't expect her to come because I hadn't thought of her for a long time. But the spirits run the show, not us. When the spirits have something to say, they come through. I became so overrun with emotion that I started crying. I asked her, "Are you okay?" The table answered by nodding and hugging me at the same time. The table creaked. I asked, "Do you want me to go see Uncle Marvin?" I tried to figure out if she had something to say to me.

Victor responded, "She said it's always good to sit down and visit."

I exclaimed, "I miss you a lot! I can't wait to tell Mom that you came through!" The table moved and made noises as closely as it could possibly get to me. I continued, "You were always so sweet and good to me when I was growing up." My Aunt Margaret had two daughters, one my age and one a year younger than me. I visited their house very often, sometimes I even spent the night. I thanked her for all that she did for me, and I told her I loved her too. Sometimes, the table responds in such a way that you just know what they are conveying. In this case, she told me that she loved me, so the table banged on the floor and moved around.

Ron asked me if she was from Arkansas, so I asked Aunt Margaret if she had a connection to Arkansas. The table didn't do anything, and Victor said she was trying to remember. I told her, "It doesn't matter. Is there something you came to tell me? If so, you can use Victor to tell me." (When the spirits go through the medium, the correspondence is much clearer.)

Victor took a deep breath and tried hard to open up to her. He said, "For one thing, she wants you to go visit someone."

I told her, "I'll take Mom to go see her brother Marvin" (Margaret's husband).

Victor said, "Her husband is kind of sad right now, and his life is at a low point." Victor paused to listen and then said, "Yes, dear." He told me, "Marvin could use some cheering up. She said it would bring a ray of sunshine into his life." The table hugged me again, and I told her I loved her too.

At this point, two pin lights appeared on Raine's chest. At first glance, everyone thought it was her necklace, but she moved the necklace aside, and the lights remained. I put my hand over the two lights to see if they would appear on my hand, and they did not. They were right over her heart! We assumed it was her dad and Sheila, sending their energy to Raine. There was no other source of light in the room.

I asked, "Margaret, if I tell Uncle Marvin about you coming to me, will he understand?"

Victor said, "If you approach the subject by saying that you had a dream about her the other night, or all of a sudden she just came to mind, he may say, 'You know I've been feeling her around too!' And he will go from there."

I asked her if she had been going to Uncle Marvin in dreams, and the table rocked back and forth and started creaking; yes, she had.

Victor said, "She has been doing more than that; she stays around him. Check with him and ask him if he has been getting any smells, or maybe a light turned on by itself. There is some way that she has been trying to reassure him. He's getting the message."

I asked, "Does he understand the messages?"

Victor answered, "He understands that she may be near him, but she wants to be careful not to scare him. Some people think that the spirits are coming for them, and she doesn't want to scare him that way. But they are things that seem familiar to him when he walks around the house, but he may not know what to make of them."

I asked her, if her son Buel Lee was there with her, but there was no response.

Victor said, "Sometimes, they have a kind of tunnel vision because they are talking directly to you." Victor took a deep breath, trying to take in what she was relaying to him. Victor then said, "She says Buel Lee is doing something somewhere else like he is in the garage doing something."

I closed by telling her I would pray for her and her whole family and asked her to give me a hug. The table just about knocked me over when it moved in to embrace me.

Victor said, "Why don't we sing 'Daisy' just to give them a little more energy ... Do you smell that? Does it smell like soap or soap powder?"

I said, "Yes, oh my gosh, it's Aunt Bea. Oh my!" I started blubbering again. I couldn't believe it. I wasn't even thinking of her at that moment, but she definitely was one spirit that I wanted to talk with. Everyone started laughing at my astonishment. I cried so hard that I couldn't speak. The table moved right up into my body and rocked back and forth, creaking loudly. I saw her light under the table, and I told her I got her clever message when she showed me the license plate that said "Ain't Bea." The table shook yes many times. I asked, "Is there any way you can show me your sweet face?" The table flipped back on its edge and started vibrating and creaking. Victor said she was sending me energy. I told her that I strive to be like her because when she was physically here, she was so successful.

Victor mentioned, "The table is grounded to the floor."

I told her, "Aunt Bea, you were a wonderful person for helping everyone in the whole family when they needed it. You gave everyone in need a place to live. I thank you from the bottom of my heart for all that you did while here. I miss you so much, and I love you a lot. It was amazing to use the smell of Tide to let me know it was you. You knew that I would recognize the smell and know you!" No one else would know this because it is something I have kept in my head all of these years. I still wash my clothes with Tide today because of her; it has such a clean smell, and it takes me back to my childhood.

The table banged against the floor as though someone laughed and slapped their knee.

I explained to the rest of the group how the smell of Tide affected me when I was small. As a single parent, my mother worked a lot; her sister—my Aunt Bea—lived within walking distance and babysat us every day. I would come home from school and sometimes enter the house through the basement door where Aunt Bea did her laundry. Once I was in the house, the smell of Tide was the first thing that got my attention, a refreshing sensation to me. My Aunt Bea lived in a huge, two-and-a-half-story, brick house, a safe haven for me. My mom, younger brother, and I always lived in an apartment. It was a big deal to me to have a yard to play in and a family situation that made me feel safe and secure. Life was completely different, when I was at Aunt Bea's house. (The whole time I talked, the table rocked back and forth, banging its top edge on the floor as if it was agreeing with me.) I told Aunt Bea, "I thought you would come through and sting Victor, and he would report that a bee had stung him. Then, I would certainly know it was you."

Victor said, "No, she chose something less painful."

I will also insert that she chose something that was a lot more persuasive to me than the bee sting. The table became so noisy that we had to talk loudly in order to hear one another. When Ron talked, the table looked around. I apologized to my Aunt Bea for not being at her funeral. My husband and I visited Las Vegas when Aunt Bea passed, and I was not told about it until we got back home. Never in my wildest dreams, would I have thought I would not be at her funeral. As my favorite aunt, we were very close. However, my faith is strong, and I am a firm believer in life after death, so I knew what to do in order to satisfy my sense of loss. I conducted my own private ceremony to honor my Aunt Bea's life and tell her how much she meant to me.

I asked Aunt Bea if she saw me when I prayed for her. The table rocked back and forth, creaking loudly. This was a yes! Ron asked me if she knew that I was writing a book and that she was going to be in that book.

I said, "Well, Aunt Bea, I am writing a book, (the table rocked and hit the floor hard, indicating that she approved), and you are going to have your own chapter in that book!" The table then went crazy and hit the floor faster and harder. It made all of us laugh at the sight of this table, expressing so much excitement. I told her that I painted my bedroom dark green because she had painted her living room the same color, and I really liked it. You might say that she is the one that inspired me to become a decorator.

Victor said, "She said okay as long as you did it for you." The table moved around rapidly over in Raine's direction.

Raine said, "Oh, hi there!"

I explained to Aunt Bea that she was my new friend, and I asked her if she liked Raine. The table, of course, answered yes. I told Aunt Bea that Raine has become like a sister to me, and it was nice because I didn't have a biological sister. The table pounded on the floor with the rocking motion. The table went up to Raine, greeted her with a hug, and then moved over to Ron. This action epitomized Aunt Bea; she would never leave anyone out. I find it quite unbelievable that the spirits can use this table as a body to express their feelings. I am so thankful that we have this séance on DVD!

Ron said, "Aunt Bea, are you from Mayberry?" His attempt at humor elicited quite a reaction from the table. It actually looked at him as if he had three heads. Ron laughed and thanked Aunt Bea for having such a great niece. The table moved in and hugged Ron. He thanked her for coming through and talking with all of us. He became very emotional over her giving him such attention. He said that he really needed the love that she emanated. Raine felt that she actually invited them to be in the family. The table moved in to hug Ron. He explained to us that he didn't have any aunts, and now he does. But what he said next got the biggest reaction of all. He said, "Hey, Aunt Bea, I do laundry too!" The table moved back quickly and fell over. Just like Fred Sanford used to grab his chest and say, "I'm coming, Elizabeth; it's a big one!" My Aunt Bea was shocked and relayed it through the table in such a hysterically funny way.

This was her true personality; she really was taken aback by the fact that a man did laundry or anything for that matter. A one woman show, Aunt Bea did everything from buying and selling houses (after she repaired them herself) to hunting deer, paying all of the bills, and handling all of the money. My Uncle Lewis had an excellent paying job, but at the end of the work week, all he did was hand his check over to his wife, and she did the rest. She invested well and made their fortune! This surprise was a very real response from my Aunt Bea as well as entertaining.

After all the laughter, I said, "I told you my Aunt Bea was a corker; you just bowled her over with that crack about you doing laundry." Everyone thanked Aunt Bea as they dried their eyes, not from tears of sadness, but from all of the laughter; no one was the same after her visit.

The guys set the table back in the original position. Victor said, "Aunt Bea is still here with us." I asked her if my older brother, Frankie, who died at seven months old was there and if she could she find him for me. The table did nothing.

Victor said, "You have to realize something; they grow up on the other side. They don't stay a baby; their souls develop. They also have the option to incarnate again, if they want to. So, he may be here on the earth again. There is no need to ask her if she sees him because he may not be recognizable."

I said, "Frankie, are you here? Can you come to me?" We all waited to see if he would come through, but he didn't.

Victor said, "Let's sing 'You Are My Sunshine.'" This is the song that we sang in the first séance that brought my grandmother through! We started singing the song, and after we finished, Victor said, "They are waiting for someone to step out of the table so the next one can step in."

I guess my Aunt Bea did not want to leave. The table moved strangely, so I asked if it was my grandma.

Victor said, "No, it's someone else."

I asked, "Is it my granddad?"

Victor said, "Hold on." The table moved around in a circle. Victor said, "Okay, you asked for someone."

I said, "Yes, I asked for Frankie. Is that you, Frankie?" The table went to Ron, and he spoke someone's name.

Victor said, "No, she [meaning me] asked for somebody." The table moved around the group, and I said with concern, "He can't find me!" Then the table charged right over and up into my body. I said, "Oh, my gosh! Is that you, Frankie?" The table nodded yes. Beside myself, I cried like a baby.

Ron said, "Okay, who is Frankie again?"

I answered, "Frankie is my older brother that died when he was only seven months old. I never got to meet him because he died before I was born, but I have always wondered about him and his whereabouts." I asked, "Frankie, do you visit Mom in dreams?

Victor said, "He is there, but he does not want to be an unpleasant reminder." Victor then added that there was gentleness there when I asked Frankie, if he was watching over Mom. Victor said, "He is watching over the whole family. He is near her, but he wants to be very gentle. He comes by and checks on everyone, and he can tell when you need him."

I asked Frankie, "Did you come to me in a dream?" The table moved into my body and hugged me. I felt like he was telling me that he loved me, so I told him that I loved him too. I told him that when he was a baby, he had a gold ring, and Mom wears that baby ring on a chain around her neck. I asked him to send her love because she needs it.

"He is saying that 'although I'm not in the physical, I am still present,'" Victor said, "I'm getting the sense that you would not recognize him today if you saw him because he is all grown up."

I replied, "Probably not." Again, I asked, "Frankie, did you come to me in a dream as a teenager?" As soon as the words were out of my mouth, I knew I made a mistake. He was older than a teenager in my dream, but I left it alone feeling that it didn't matter and said nothing else. But just as miraculous as this séance had been thus far, it proved to be more so when Victor spoke his next words.

Victor said, "He is saying that he came to you as someone in his twenties." There is no possible way that Victor could have known this, it is something that only I knew.

"Yes, yes, Frankie that was you standing by my bedside looking down at me!" I replied in astonishment. The table nodded yes. "And you were wearing a Letterman's jacket," I continued. The table nodded again, even before I finished speaking. Overemotional, I had a hard time controlling my tears as well as my voice because of the lump in my throat. I have thought about Frankie throughout my whole life and often wondered where he was—if he reincarnated and was back here in the physical, or if he was moving on and learning on the other side. Now, I finally had a chance to communicate with him. *How awesome is this!*

Victor said, "He is at a point where he likes where he is, and he wants you to recognize him as a man in his twenties, instead of the infant he was when he crossed over."

I explained to Victor and the others that I woke up one night out of a sound sleep and saw this young guy standing at the side of my bed looking down at me. With his hair styled in a fifties fashion, kind of like James Dean and clad in a letterman's jacket, he stood with his chin resting on his fist Jack-Benny style with a gold graduation ring on his finger. For years, I tried to figure out who this young man was. Now, I know without a doubt that it was my brother Frankie. I said, "You kind of look like someone from high school, right, Frankie?"

Victor interrupted and said, "I don't mean to be disrespectful, but he looks more like Fonzerelli." Everyone laughed, but I knew Victor was right!

I said, "Yeah, that's how he appeared to me." Just then I was reminded of my younger brother Larry because that is how Larry always tried to be—cool. I asked Frankie if he would watch over Larry and send him love and if he could help us get back together because I haven't seen or spoken to my brother Larry in over eight years. I saw a light under the table; Victor told us earlier that this is the spirits' energy. I then said, "I love you, Frankie, and thank you for coming to me."

Victor said, "He has watched over you for all of these years."

I replied, "Have you really? Oh, my gosh!" The table moved in and hugged me. I told him I would pray for his soul and tell Mom that he came to me.

Victor said, "Well, it's going to be how she takes it."

I said, "Is it okay if I tell her?" The table nodded yes.

Victor said, "Okay." The table moved in a different manner, and I asked Frankie what he was doing.

Ron said, "If they grow up on the other side, they have to be purely innocent."

Victor took in a deep breath as he tried to receive the answer to Ron's statement. He said, "Okay, here's what I'm getting. He is saying we don't have the chance to give in to temptation, but that doesn't mean we still can't be cool!" Everyone laughed, and the table started thumping on the floor loudly as though Frankie laughed with us.

I asked Frankie if he saw my boys, Troy and Rodney, and my grandkids and said, "Aren't they great?" The table rocked and creaked loudly as I requested that he watch over them for me. The table at this point moaned and moved back to look at me; it was so incredible. Victor said he stepped back to look at the whole family. I asked for his help in the circumstances surrounding my family. The table moaned and groaned in response to my request. I thanked Frankie for coming through to me and explained to him that I really needed him to come to me.

Although I'm sure Frankie already knew that, Victor said, "Listen to the noise that table is making. No one can make the table make noises like that!" At this point, the guys set the table back up and into its original position. I was completely exhausted when Frankie's energy stepped out of the table. Because I was breathing hard, Victor told me to drink plenty of water when I got out of the séance because we were using a lot of plasmic energy.

The table spun right away. This time it was for Ron. His friend and partner, Art Ross, took his turn at coming through.

Victor said, "There is so much energy in the room that all of the spirits are just lined up, waiting for their chance to come through. Look at the pools of lighted energy on the floor behind you." Victor seemed quite amazed.

Ron started talking to Art and asked him about the day that he died. Ron said that he tried to talk to Art, but he just blew him off. Something or someone told Ron that Art did not want Ron to see him die because Art had seen Ron die so many times before in previous lifetimes. Ron asked Art, "Is that true?"

Victor said, "First off, if you saw him die that thought would be in your mind all of your life, and he did not want that to be there." The table nodded affirmatively. Victor continued, "Art did not mean to be disrespectful to you; he just wanted you to remember the way he used to be instead of at death.

Ron then asked Art if he, Mark, Raine, and I had been connected in previous lifetimes. The table did nothing, so Ron then asked Art to go to the person that had been with the two of them before in a previous life. The table did a marvelous thing; it raced to each and every one of us, pushed up into our bodies, and scared us half to death—no pun intended. Ron asked if Victor had also been with us. The table turned on its side and rocked hard. I asked Raine to watch her knees because I didn't want the table to crash down on her legs. If you remember, in Chapter Twenty, Séance 1, this is a 100 lb wooden table, moving around as a person would.

Ron said he had to ask, "You have been involved with me on these projects that I have been working on since 1989. People are now telling me that the funding is ready to happen; is it?" The table moved erratically and nodded yes.

Victor said, "There is a mere formality before you get the funding."

Ron said to Art, "I am going to put your name on one of the buildings in the projects. Do you approve of that?" The table nodded yes and creaked. Ron asked Art if he had met his grandfather Jake.

Victor asked Ron what his grandfather's skill was, and Ron said he was a farmer and the mayor of the town for over sixty years. Art put Ron's grandfather Jake through, and the table moved up to Ron's body. Ron said, "You said you trusted my instincts, Jake. Do you still trust them?" Raine asked Jake if he was present at her reading in Casadaga, and the table nodded; yes, he was. Ron then said to his grandpa, "Grandpa Jake, you have been on my mind a lot. Is Grandma Stella there too?" The table creaked but did not answer his question.

Victor said, "She's there." Victor stopped to listen to what they were telling him, while Ron said she was a quiet soul. They set the table back up right. Victor said there was so much enthusiasm. The spirits can sense the energy and get a rush from all of our energy.

Ron asked about his Grandpa George and stated that he had a picture of his grandpa when he was still in diapers, hanging on a clothesline. Ron said that his Grandpa George was a dark man; he looked like George Jr. He asked Grandpa Jake if he could create a connection with his Grandpa George, since he lost contact with him. Victor tried to reach for the answer by taking a deep breath and concentrating but could not get what Ron looked for. Ron said, "That's okay, I have always needed Grandpa Jake's approval, and I got it."

The spirit seemed to leave, and Victor immediately questioned, "Who passed from something in their stomach?" I immediately knew my Uncle James was back, and the first thing I did was apologize for taking the conversation away from Ron and his family. Little did I know that my Uncle James was back to speak to Ron. I knew that he wanted to tell me something in the first séance, but I was so sidetracked that I was unavailable to him. Now, here he was again, making a second attempt to talk to me.

Victor said, "Okay, James, hang on." Victor said that Grandpa Jake stepped aside, so that Uncle James could step in. He said there are two people there with him. Victor asked me, if he had sinus trouble too, and I answered, "Yes, probably." Victor asked me if James died of an illness or if it was an accident. It could have been both; I wasn't sure. I just knew that he went into the hospital with stomach trouble, and he wasn't supposed to die. Victor said, "Was this a car accident or something that crushed him?"

I said, "No, nothing like that."

Victor said, "Is it like he had an allergic reaction or something because I'm choking on something; it's almost like anaphylaxis. My head hurts."

I replied, "So, he was allergic to something they gave him like penicillin or something?"

Victor answered, "Yeah."

Mark said, "So, is this James?"

I said, "Yeah, it is. Hi, Uncle James, I love you! You came back to tell me didn't you that you had a reaction to a medicine that they gave you?"

Victor said, "Something burst in his stomach but that still wouldn't cause all of this from the head and nose, but if you are allergic to something, you go into anaphylactic shock, and all of a sudden your lungs and your brain fill with fluid."

I asked about his son Jimmy, and if he was there with him.

Mark cut in and said, "Well, did he have a message for you?"

I said, "I thought that was it." So, I asked Uncle James if that, in fact, was the message that he was trying to convey to me, so that I could tell the family.

Victor opened his mouth to speak and then started laughing, "He is funny! Yes, inquiring minds want to know."

I said, "Yes, he was always funny."

Victor said, "It started out in his stomach, and then it spread. Has it been a while since he has passed?"

"Yes, it has," I responded.

Victor said, "More then twenty years?"

And I said, "Oh, yeah. He died in the 1970s."

Victor said, "He is saying it's something that they didn't realize and something that they didn't know; they didn't have enough knowledge of this side effect or something like that.

"I asked Uncle James, "Does Pat [his daughter] have the same stomach problems that you had." Nothing!

Victor said, "No, he didn't get a sense of that." Victor struggled to understand the rest of the message. He continued, "Okay, who has something that is below the stomach that is bothering them? Like gastritis or of the colon or something?"

Raine and Ron said at the same time, "Ron's dad."

Victor said, "No, you asked if he had another message."

I said, "Yeah, maybe it's me. Are you talking about me, Uncle James?"

Victor said, "He is using his passing as a matrix for something else."

I said again, "Your daughter Pat does she have that?" Once again, there was no response.

Victor said, "No, that's not it."

Mark said, "The table is going to Ron." It moved in closer to Ron.

Victor said, "If you can believe this, James is here to give Ron the message. Is it like IBS (Irritable Bowel Syndrome)?" Ron started talking about his dad again and Victor said, "No, he is showing me something that is happening in the present that I've no knowledge of. Okay, a spirit will do that." I asked Uncle James if it was with Ron. There was no response. Victor said, "Okay, so your father has the colon cancer; okay, are you irritable?"

Ron finally said, "Yes, right now, I am."

Victor told him to watch what's irritating him. "Do you work around any chemicals, or are you working around something that you might be absorbing?" Victor questioned. Ron answered no. Victor said, "Okay, because it is something that is going into you. It is a combination of things; you've got the psychological factor, and then you've got something in your diet. They are showing me little plastic stringy things, fiber. Are you getting enough fiber?"

Ron replied, "No, I don't get enough fiber."

Victor continued, "I would suggest that you get some more fiber in your diet. You want to be smooth and gentle on your intestinal system. I'm not a doctor; I can't prescribe, but I'm getting the message from him for you. He's telling you to get more fiber in your diet with salads, or maybe if you want to take a fiber tablet."

Then, there was a strange noise like a drip. Victor said "Who did that? Did you hear that?" Yes, we all heard the sound but could not discern where it came from. So, Victor said, "Okay, thank you, we will take that as a yes. I'm getting a sense that he wants you to smooth your intestines. Remember how our grandparents used to tell us to drink a little fat or something to oil our insides?" The table nodded affirmatively.

Ron said, "I quit taking my Omega oil. James, do I need to go have a Colonoscopy? I'm 58 years old, and I've put it off."

I interjected, "You know what, I've had it done twice; it does not hurt, and it's a great peace of mind to have it done."

Victor said, "I don't get a sense of it being life or death. I just get that it will be soothing for you."

Ron said, "Well, I have corrected everything else that has been a problem for me health-wise. It's the only thing I have left. Thank you, Uncle James!"

Victor said, "The thing with your business is that there is just one little formality; it's not a big thing, but it's eating you up inside. You are getting yourself all inflamed and distressed. You don't have to."

Mark said, "You see, that's the message we were waiting for."

I said, "He tried to tell us this last time we were here. I knew there was a message, so I left the door open. I even prayed to Uncle James to come through if he had a message for me, and I would give him my utmost attention this time."

Ron said something to the effect that our families were connected on the other side. Mark interjected that Ron gained an aunt and an uncle. I said, "My family is your family."

Victor said, "Hey, listen, speaking as a medium, when you marry somebody, their family still hangs around you because you were in the family. So when I'm trying to read for someone, I look for reassurance that they know who or what I'm talking about, and they say something like, oh, that could have been my second or third husband's mother. Golly gee, that can get confusing."

The whole time that we talked, the table never stopped moving and creaking. I asked Uncle James if there was anything else he had to tell me.

Victor replied, "No, he is stepping out."

We all felt drained after Uncle James came through, so we took a deep breath to recuperate. Mark commented that Grandpa Jake brought Uncle James through to give Ron the message about his health. Ron said that his Grandpa Jake shot the table right into his stomach three times, when he came in to talk to him.

Victor said, "Okay, what's the point?"

Ron said, "That he is strong!"

Victor said, "No-o-o, the point is for you to check out your stomach problems!" Time lapsed; it seemed like no one else was going to come through. During this time, I prayed that Mark's Grandpa Kralemann or Grandma Yust would come through.

Victor did some deep breathing and concentrated at this point, trying to get the next spirit to come through. We waited for what seemed like five minutes. Finally, Victor said, "Okay, this is going to sound a little funny. Let's sing 'Jingle Bells.' They seem to love that song." This seemed like an odd choice of song, but it fit when the next spirit did come through. We waited for the spirit to make itself known as the table started moving in a circle. Victor then said, "There are two people here; it's for you, sir," indicating Mark.

I thought I knew who it was. When Victor said there where two people, I was sure it was Grandpa Kralemann and Grandma Yust. My guess was close; everyone was extremely surprised as to who they were.

Victor said, "One is a very strong man." When he said this, the table moved in a wide, sweeping motion, pushing us all back in our chairs. Victor said, "Please don't take this the wrong way, but it's almost like he wants to slap you upside the head and say it's not hard!"

Mark immediately recognized it as being his Grandpa Yust. He started speaking with him, "So, what do you think about all of this stuff we are doing in Florida? That's where you were at, pretty cool, huh?" The table moved and creaked. Mark continued, "How do you like the house in Naples?"

Victor asked, "Do you see the house in Naples?" He relayed, "Yes, he goes with you everywhere you go."

Mark said he was following in his grandpa's footsteps by starting up all these companies, and the table acknowledged his remark. Mark said," He loves boats too; he was a boater." The table started going to everyone of us as if to include us in the conversation. Mark said, "I knew you were along for the ride; I've always felt you there."

Victor said, "There are two people there."

Mark said, "Is my other grandpa there too?" Mark said that his grandpa was a big powerful man like Ron's grandpa Jake. I inserted that he was a Virgo too and a very intelligent guy. Mark added, "Don't get in his way!"

Victor remarked, "Real humble too, right?"

We all laughed. Mark said he was a tall and a real good-looking man. The table thumped hard on the floor in agreement. Mark stated, "When Grandpa spoke, the world stopped to listen."

Ron added, "Just like Jake." The table went crazy by thumping, rocking, and spinning. We all laughed. I asked Grandpa Yust if he came to Mark in a dream and outlined how to proceed in his business matters. The table nodded affirmatively.

The table then got up into Raine's face, and she said, "Whoa, hi!"

Mark said he has always felt his grandpa's presence. I know that it was very reassuring for Mark that his grandpa came through.

Victor said, "I am smelling Vitalis hair cream. When he was alive, did he use hair cream or something like that?"

Mark said he always wore his hair slicked back. Mark asked him if he hangs out and watches Frankie (Mark's uncle, his grandpa's son) in Florida. The table stopped moving but continued to make popping sounds. We asked Grandpa about his passing, if he just suddenly left.

Victor said, "'The meter was up,' he said." The table confirmed what Victor said. Mark asked if Grandma Yust was there with him. Victor said, "Again, people are in different places." Mark was positive that Grandpa Yust would come through today. We thanked him for coming through, just as we did all of the other spirits. Mark told him, "I am so happy that you are going to be on this adventure with us. I knew that there was a huge connection between Ron and our families."

Victor said, "There is a common message that all of these people are telling you; for one thing, don't get in over your head. You can get involved in so much that you can swamp yourself. Go step by step, so that you get—" Victor stopped here and asked them, "Okay, what are you showing me? Gosh, I've got both gentlemen, the farmer and him, both grandpas' hands over my hand. They are both saying, 'Do not put more in the hand, then you can shove in your mouth.' It's a symbolic message to not choke on it. In other words, they are saying, 'Don't bite off more than you can chew.' Slow down and don't get crazy."

Mark said, "So, I've got to really slow Ron down."

Victor answered, "You can't eat more than he (Ron) can digest." Along with all of our laughter, came laughter from the other side in the form of the table thumping on the floor. Once again, it was like a slap on the knee. It was quite unbelievable. Victor said, "Both gentlemen were like a balance scale, each one of them is trying to balance the two of you in this project."

The guys picked the table up to set in pick into position. Victor used Raine as an example in his next statement. He said, "Oh please, ma'am, don't be insulted when I say that you fell because you were not watching where you were walking, or you were not careful of the situation."

(That is exactly what happened prior to the séance. The four of us went out for breakfast, and while we were walking into the restaurant, Raine tripped on the curb and fell flat on her face. She caught herself with both hands, so that her face would not hit the pavement, but all of a sudden, her face was shoved to the pavement by an invisible hand; the three of us watched it happen.)

Victor continued, "It's kind of the same between the two of you, so make sure that you maintain your balance, so that you don't knock anything out of kilter." Raine was a little bewildered by the spirits picking on her. Victor assured her that they were not picking on her but taking advantage of a situation to get their point across to Ron and Mark. Then the table did a rather strange thing, it went up to hug Raine, and we didn't know what to make of it, but then Victor said that they were apologizing to her. Mark spoke up to say that we have been getting messages for about six weeks to be patient on this project.

Then Victor asked, "Who was the math whiz? They are showing me that this, plus this, plus this, equals this. And this is not going to happen here, if you do not have that back there. And it is not going to come out right. This spirit is showing me to go through one step at a time, like four plus five is nine, then nine plus something is something else. Don't miss any steps. This spirit is showing me these numbers for a reason! Four plus five is nine!"

Ron then stated that there are nine guys in the group. While we were trying to figure out the numbers, Victor said, "Actually, it is eleven."

I said, "They are showing you eleven? Wow!" I was amazed and pleased because eleven is a power number in numerology.

Victor said, "Eleven is a master number. You know you might not get it as an eleven if you didn't get it as a nine first."

Ron said, "Maybe it means that the nine of us need to look at it twice for it to add up to an eleven." Victor seemed to agree with Ron that maybe that was it. I didn't agree with the analogy then, and I still don't agree now. I think the missing number two is in the form of people. I believe that we need to add two more people to the group!

Victor said, "Not only because of the numerology aspect of it, but it puts you in the position you need to be in."

I brought up that maybe we should add more people, but Ron said, "No, we were going to add that CEO, but we decided to look at it collectively twice." He was adamant, so I dropped it. Victor said he saw papers or blueprints, "This does not make sense to me; this corner of the building or this juncture right here does not look right." Victor added, "It's going to be someone else that sees it." We never once mentioned to Victor that we were building anything, only that we had this project.

Victor said, "As a finale, we'll sing 'She'll Be Coming Around the Mountain.' Let's sing with a whole lot of enthusiasm because it helps to build up a lot of energy for whatever they may want to do." We started singing in a fun-loving way to give the spirits as much energy as possible. Victor said someone had been standing in the back of the room because he could see two puddles of ectoplasm.

He asked us if we wanted to see if the spirits could raise the table over our heads just as we attempted to do in the first séance. Of course we did, so we all stood with our hands still placed lightly on top of the table. We counted to four, and the table began to rise over our heads to where Raine and I could not touch the tabletop any longer. As it began its descent, Ron said, "Slowly, slowly, slowly," concerned that it would come crashing down to the floor. We were ecstatic! We had never seen that before or been a part of something so phenomenal.

Victor said, "Let's try it one more time." Once again, we counted to four, and the table rose faster than before as we said, "Up, up, up!" Then, the table came back down. All of us were blown away. We sat back down to close our session, and the table moved again as another spirit proceeded to come though. We said, "Oh, you're not done?" We were speaking, of course, to the spirits.

Victor recognized that it was a spirit coming though for him and asked, "Is that you, Jim?" The table nodded yes, and Victor explained that Jim used to be his best friend and that he had headed all of the séance classes. *Did Jim cause the puddles of ectoplasm that Victor saw in the back of the room?* Victor continued, "Jim, you know what's happening tonight. Will you be with Ester and help her?" The table thumped on the floor, indicating yes. Victor asked Jim if he could send Ester some healing energy, stating that she needed it badly. The table again thumped, thumped, and thumped. Victor asked Jim if her problem was a pinched nerve or something of that sort. He asked again for his assistance and protection with whatever was happening that evening. When Victor spoke with Jim, we were not always sure of the answers because it seemed like a private conversation. Victor asked if Jim was going to inspire the speaking tonight and then said, "Okay, I'll just watch what I say then." We laughed at the warning that Victor received from his old friend. The table started tapping extremely fast on the floor for a very long time (kind of like a squeaky swing). Victor asked what he was saying. The table loudly and adamantly intended to make sure that Victor received the message correctly. Victor said, "It's not what? It's not to say something?" The table stopped dead (no pun intended). Victor continued to question, "It's about what somebody else says? It's not what you think is wrong with Ester?" The table started up again, rocking back and forth and creaking like a porch swing. Then it stopped suddenly, and Victor said, "It's not anybody doing Voodoo?" The table was silent as was Victor. Victor said, "Okay, a shot of cortisone or steroids will help it?" The table creaked (spoke), and then Victor answered, "Okay, if it's something else, can you intercede or help stop it?" Once again, total silence from the table. Victor then replied, "Well, you'll be with us tonight then; okay, I want to thank you for the encouragement." The table radiated energy toward Victor. He confirmed that he needed the energy and asked for Jim to send healing energy again to Ester. Again, the table started rocking and creaking rapidly. Victor started smelling incense of some sort. Victor thanked his buddy and told him that he would tell Ester that Jim would be there with them tonight. Victor said that Jim married Ester and him, and they were married on Jim's anniversary.

Victor instructed us to hold hands and begin reciting the closing prayer. We thanked the spirits for the wonderful messages that we received and asked for guidance, so that we could put the information to good use. Victor stopped and then said, "'End the sermon,' they are saying. Okay, give us what it is we need to know. All right, we close the doors for communication; we shut the gates. Those that are here and wish to stay with us, you have our permission, and we thank you for all the help and guidance that you give us on a constant basis. Those spirits that have to go somewhere else to learn their lessons and appointed tasks, we release you with light and love and thank you for coming. Now, we return this room to be better energetically than when we came." We finished by singing "Happy Trails," one of Jim's songs.

Victor added, "Now, in closing, dear God, we ask that You be with these wonderful loving people in their journey; always keep them in Your Hands and under the wings of your Angels. And this we ask in Your Name, Amen."

This picture is of the séance room in Colby Temple. Because the spirits are no longer in the physical, they use the wooden table to communicate. As bizarre as it may sound, the spirits display their emotions by enabling the table to flip on its side (tops edge), make popping and creaking sounds, nod and even levitate over our heads.

Raine's sister, Sheila, came through during the second
séance. Raine, desperately needed to hear from her sister,
and know that she was okay and in a much better place. It
is our belief, that Raine's father, Bud (also deceased),
helped Sheila come through.

What a pleasant surprise to have my Aunt Margaret come through so unexpectedly. While I loved her dearly, I hadn't thought about her for sometime. In 1980, two weeks before Christmas, my Aunt Margaret and Uncle Marvin had this picture taken. Margaret died on Feb. 25,

In honor of their fiftieth wedding anniversary, my Aunt Bea and Uncle Lewis had this picture made for the family. Aunt Bea was one of the strongest and most generous women I have ever known, and I miss herdearly. She taught me how to live, love and laugh! Uncle Lewis passed on November 14, 1991, and Aunt Bea joined him on August 4, 1999.

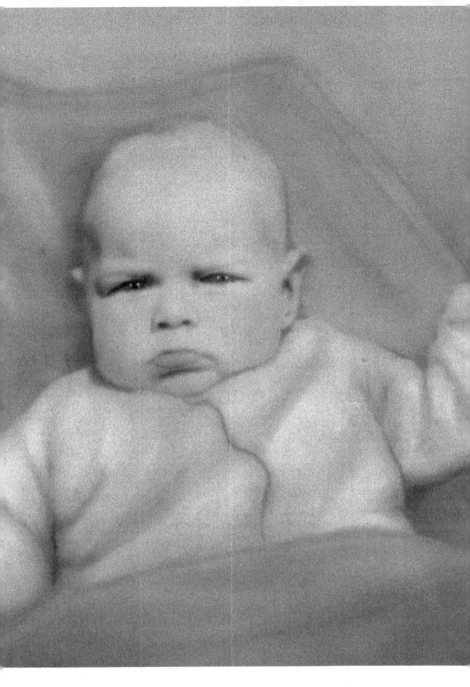

Frankie Joe Hawkins, my brother, was only seven months old when he died. Born on October 12, 1946, he died on May 14, 1947.

Frank Yust, my husband's grandfather, was a very powerful man. He started his own waste management company with just one truck, and it became the largest company of its kind in the mid-west.

24

Pennies from Heaven

June 25, 2007

O ur trip to Florida was a short one, only a week long. We spent most of our time conducting business, but finally, I had a chance to do as I pleased, so I went shopping. I dropped by Nature's Garden, a natural food/herb store, to pick up a few items, when I spied a product that I thought might help my mother. She experienced pain and numbness in her legs and feet for sometime due to a pinched nerve. Although she saw a chiropractor, had acupuncture, and even met several times with a physical therapist, the problems persisted. I purchased the product hoping that it might help relieve some of her pain. When I left the market to drive home, I decided to call my mother on my cell phone to tell her about the homeopathic remedy.

My mother recently sold her home and is in the process of moving in with my husband and me until the three of us relocate to Naples, Florida. We plan to live in Naples half of the year and spend the other half of the year at our home in St. Louis. The purpose of this short trip to Naples was to check on some investment properties and to look around for a home for my mother. She will turn eighty-three in November of 2008 and is still in excellent health, so she is quite excited about this move.

I dialed my mother's number. When she answered the phone, she was out of breath. I asked her what she was doing. She informed me that she had been packing, and it was a good time to take a break. My mother has a tendency to overdo things until her body reminds her that she is not a spring chicken anymore. When she gets excited about something, she tends to talk fast and continuously, so it's hard to get a word in and when you do, she rarely hears it. I find myself having to raise my voice and say, "Mom! Mom! Are you listening to me?" She will most always say, "H-m-m-m-m?" in a childlike manner that makes it hard to get angry with her. I managed to tell her about the nerve medicine and ask her about her garage sale. When moving, it is always a good idea to get rid of as much stuff as you can BEFORE you move! So, you end up selling, giving away, donating, and leaving behind all of the stuff you have accumulated over the years. Well, this conversation with my mother took all of twenty-five minutes, the time it took for me to drive home from the market.

When I pulled into my garage, my mother still talked about her garage sale. Mom's voice suddenly changed, and I heard her say, "Linda, what is it with all of these pennies?"

I waited for a few seconds just to see if she really wanted an answer, or if she was going to continue to talk. When it seemed liked it was an honest question, I posed my question to her, "What exactly do you mean, Mom?"

She said, "I am finding pennies everywhere I go; it's getting pretty weird! When we were cleaning up after the sale, I found a penny under the carport, and then Ruth [my aunt] found one in the driveway."

I said, "Well, Mom it's not that unusual to find money on the ground after you just have a garage sale."

She said, "No, it's not, but I'm finding them everywhere. Don't you remember the day we closed on my house, and you drove into the gas station to fuel up, and you went inside to get us a couple of drinks and on the way, you found a penny on the ground? When you came back out you said there was another penny in same place of the one you picked up?"

I said, "Yeah, that was pretty weird!"

She continued, "I have been finding pennies for over a month. It's getting silly."

I told her that I have read on a number of occasions that our deceased loved ones often put objects in our paths to remind us that they are still around us. I continued, "Maybe this is Uncle Buel or Uncle James trying to get your attention."

She said she didn't know and kept right on talking about how odd it was. I asked her if there was a connection to her family and a penny, something that may have happened when she was younger.

She told me a story that I had not heard before, "Well, one time when I was little, I did the dishes, and Mom gave me a penny as a reward. I asked her if I could have a penny every time I did the dishes, and she said, 'Now don't get that notion in your head!'"

I exclaimed, "There you go, Mom! It's Grandma. She wants you to know that she is still here with you."

When I thought about it, it made a lot of sense to me. Mom packed away all of her photographs, except for one frame of six photos. They were all of my grandma and granddad. She left it sitting out as long as she could, and then when we brought her things to my house, she held it in her hands during the drive home. Once home, I placed the photo on her nightstand and told her that I really missed Grandma. Mom said she missed her a lot too. So maybe it was Grandma's way of saying, "I am still right there beside you!"

June 26, 2007

I called Mom again to check on her and told her that I had mentioned her penny saga to our friends, Ron and Raine, and they thought it was an amazing story. She told me that it had not stopped happening. She said that as she reached down to pick up her purse, her wallet fell out onto the bed, and the change dumped out all over the bed. She picked up all of her monies and put them back into the wallet. As she started to return the wallet back into her purse, she looked down and saw that a penny had landed on her blouse and stuck there. Way to go, Grandma! She had also taken her car in for an oil change, and as she sat in the waiting room, another penny popped up. Mom sat in a chair with wooden arms. She walked over to the end table to exchange magazines. But when she sat back down, she felt something on the arm of the chair. She lifted her arm to see what it was, and when she did, a penny stuck to her arm. This kind of stuff scares Mom—as it may several people—but I find it awesome!

Later that same evening, we went out to dinner with Ron and Raine. It was our last night in Naples, and we planned to spend the evening with them. We ate at a restaurant called The Boat House and then walked around the docks, looking at all of the boats that were for sale. Ron and Raine walked side by side in front of us. Mark and I walked about a foot apart. As I glanced down, I spotted something strange. I bent down to pick it up, and as I did, I noticed that it was a dollar bill folded neatly into a square. I instantly knew that it was a sign from Grandma. No, it was not a penny, but 100 pennies, folded neatly into a tiny square. To me, it said, "Thank you for explaining to your mother that it was me, your Grandma, trying to tell her that I am still with her, and I do see everything that is happening in her life."

You may recall in Chapter Twenty, Séance, the conversation that I had with my grandmother about my mother. We had been estranged from each other for a while, and it has been difficult at times for us to relate to one another. My grandmother told Victor that she would be the bridge to connect us back together. For whatever part she played, I sincerely thank her. I loved my grandma dearly as she was a very important part of my life, and I will always remember her caring ways. As for my mother, she will never know the extent of my love for her. Yes, I do a lot for her, and she appreciates what I do, but she does not always understand what I say or do. She sometimes misinterprets what is said, and it can be days or even weeks before she speaks. My mother gets things into her head and tends to make up her own conclusions about what has happened. I know this about her, and the fact that she is not very well-educated or sophisticated helps me to overlook much of what she says or does. I do love my mother dearly, and I intend to make every moment of our lives together into the best memories possible.

It is always an amazing feeling when you stumble upon an item that was meant to convey a message, especially from the other side. If you are like me, it may take some time to sink in before you have that light-bulb moment. Either way, I don't think time is an issue on the other side, and I don't think our loved ones give up on us easily. If they have an important message to tell us, I am sure they have many ways of executing that message and will get our attention no matter what it takes.

My mother and I during Christmas of 2006.

25

Foyer Guest

————July 9, 2007————

On a Sunday night, Mark, Mom, Evans, and I played cards in the lower level of the house. We had finished dinner and decided to entertain ourselves with a friendly card game. Mom had just moved into our house and was living on the lower level where we do most of our entertaining.

Normally, Mom retires for the evening around eight o'clock. However, she was having so much fun that she managed to stay awake and in the game until around ten, which just so happened to be when she lost. She kissed everyone good night and went to bed in her lower-level bedroom.

We continued playing cards into the night. Mark was the next player to go out, which left Evans, my ferocious competitor, and me to battle it out. For those of you who aren't that competitive, let me tell you that we absolutely live to do one another in. Finally, the game ended around midnight with yours truly as the winner! Evans said good night and went upstairs to let himself out as Mark and I proceeded to finish cleaning up the downstairs kitchen before we retired for the evening. We heard Evans as he walked across the living room, the upstairs kitchen, and out of the house. About five to ten minutes later, Mark and I headed upstairs to our bedroom.

We sleepily climbed the stairs, and as we reached the top, we both stopped abruptly. We spotted parts of my floral arrangement in the living room, lying in the foyer a couple of feet away. We looked at each other questioningly and said, "What happened?" We knew that Evans went straight to the garage and did not stop, or we would have heard him. However, I did decide to call him to ensure that he did not attempt to play a joke on us. I waited the five minutes that I knew it would take him to get home from our house before I dialed his number. After the five minutes, I called his house and asked him if he noticed anything strange in the house as he left.

He said, "No, I didn't. It was dark when I went upstairs because there were no lights on. Why do you ask?" I explained to him what Mark and I found when we went upstairs.

He exclaimed, "No way, take a picture so that I can see it before you pick anything up."

I told him that I would, and we then tried to make sense of how the flowers arrived at that particular location. *If it was possible for the flowers to fall out of the tall vase sitting on the floor, wouldn't they be strung out from the rest of the flowers in the vase to the floor in a scattered array? Or wouldn't the whole vase of flowers be tipped over?* From the way the flowers lay on the foyer rug, it looked as though they were grabbed with two hands out of the vase and positioned on the floor. After talking to Evans on the phone, I decided to leave the flowers laying there for a few days or at least until Evans could see them for himself.

Before going to sleep, Mark and I discussed the subject further. I asked Mark what he thought, and he said, "Linda, there is only one explanation as to how the flowers ended up on the floor like that!" I knew that he was speaking about our resident spirits and that he was dead serious—no pun intended. I also knew that the spirits that live with us have a bizarre sense of humor. I just couldn't figure out what they were trying to tell us, or why they rearranged the flowers. Maybe they were just playing around. I'm sure of one thing; if they do have a message for us, they will not stop trying to get our attention until we get the message.

In order to shed more light into the foyer, this picture was taken the next morning. As you can see, it is a little hard to believe that the maroon reeds just fell out of the flower vase, and landed where they are laying. But this is exactly how we found them, when we came upstairs.

Author Biographical Note

For the past twenty-five years Linda and her husband have owned and operated their own Event Planning/Rental business in the St. Louis area. Being the creative side of the business Linda has produced several successful events for the affluent in the area, including Anheuser Busch, American Airline, AT & T, The Rams Organization as well as many, many others. After years in marketing, creating costumes, weddings and special events, Linda has decided to pursue her passions for writing. While still in school, Linda began writing poetry and continued doing so through out her early adulthood, until unusual events started taking place in her life. As each phenomenon occurred, Linda began keeping journals of the events and sharing them with friends and family. Amused by the stories, others began to coax her into putting them into book form and having them published. Years later, she decided to do just that by creating what is now known as "Did That Just Happen?"

While Linda and her husband still call St. Louis, Mo. their home base, they spend the winter months in Naples, Florida. A wife, mother of two and grandmother of five, Linda enjoys life to the fullest and hopes she has many years to enjoy her passion for writing.

Author Biographical Note

Printed in the United States
by Baker & Taylor Publisher Services